Real Peace,
Real Security

FACETS

Selected Titles in the Facets Series

Real Peace, Real Security

The Challenges of Global Citizenship

Sharon D. Welch

Fortress Press
Minneapolis

REAL PEACE, REAL SECURITY
The Challenges of Global Citizenship

Cover image: © Purestock/Getty Images
Author photo: Seanan Holland

Library of Congress Cataloging-in-Publication Data
Welch, Sharon D.
  Real peace, real security : the challenges of global citizenship / Sharon
D. Welch.
    p. cm. – (Facets series)
  Includes bibliographical references.
  ISBN 978-0-8006-6279-0 (alk. paper)
  1. Nonviolence–Moral and ethical aspects. 2. Peace–Moral and ethi-
cal aspects. 3. Globalization–Moral and ethical aspects. I. Title.
  BJ1459.5.W44 2008
  172'.42–dc22

                         2008038751

Manufactured in the U.S.A.
12   11   10   09   08   1   2   3   4   5   6   7   8   9   10

Contents

For Jon

Foreword

Peacemaking
and Human Rights

William F. Schulz

Mine is a wintry view of life, by which I mean very simply that I am deeply cynical about human nature, including my own. Perhaps that is not surprising given my twelve years of experience as executive director of Amnesty International USA, with its corresponding exposure to brutality and war.

As one who was required on a daily basis for those twelve years to hear about the most sordid and gratuitous violence, who met with some regularity those who had been the victims of it—twelve-year-old girls, for example, blinded and facially scarred for life because they had disappointed their fifty-year-old husbands to whom their parents in southeast Asia had sold them and whose husbands had therefore thrown carbolic acid in their faces—and who has visited the filthy prisons of Liberia and trod the refugee camps of Darfur, I am not easily convinced that humans, in the words of Psalm 8, are "but a little lower than the angels."

A South African neuropsychologist has recently the-
orized that cruelty, especially in males, is grounded in
an adaptive reaction from the Paleozoic era when early
humans were predators and had to hunt for their food;
that the appearance of pain and blood in the prey was
a signal of triumph; and that gradually the evocation of
such reactions—howls of pain, the appearance of blood—
in our fellow humans became associated with personal
and social power, with the success of the hunt.[1] That
strikes me as about right. Call it Calvinism, if you like;
dismiss original sin if you must; attribute it to a male
gene if you feel so inclined; but in this respect I think
eighteenth-century theology was far closer to the mark
than much of contemporary liberalism: left unchecked,
human beings are vicious sons of bitches with whom
you would be very wise not to leave your two-year-old
or your credit cards.

So what this means is that if we are to live in a world
even occasionally at peace, we must create structures
and norms that discourage the appearance of our basest
impulses. Some of those are cultural, some are legal,
and some—ironically enough—entail the judicious use
of force. These latter, in other words, entail indulging
our baser impulses in order to stop other people from
indulging theirs.

The cultural ways in which we can decrease violence
are not simple, but they are straightforward: building
self-esteem, for example; teaching conflict resolution;
boycotting violent media. I'm not going to elaborate
upon these options, but I in no way underestimate their
importance. What I want to address are the legal and
military options, for they are the nub of the issue. Let's
take the legal first.

Southern segregationists were wrong about everything, but one thing they were indisputably wrong about

was their oft-repeated slogan, "Ya cain't legislate morality." Well, not only *can* you legislate morality; legislating morality is one of the major ways to change moral standards. Today's conservatives know that, which is one reason they are so afraid of laws permitting marriage between people of the same gender. Not because of the so-called sanctity of marriage, but because they know that few things will have a greater impact on changing social norms about homosexuality than if gay and lesbian people are recognized legally as marital partners. Within a generation of that happening across this country, controversy about the morality of same-sex relations will be, if not a thing of the past, radically diminished. This is how most value changes take place.

Why do most people obey laws even though they know they probably won't get caught if they don't? Why, for example, do most of us wear seat belts today even when we have little, if any, fear that we might be arrested for breaking the seat belt laws? One answer of course is that we know wearing seat belts may save our lives. But I am old enough to remember when seat belts were first installed in cars, and I remember quite clearly that for many years they sat unused despite the fact that we all knew that using them was in our best interests. What changed over the years such that the use of seat belts today is almost *pro forma*?

First, the culture changed, thanks to Ralph Nader and others whose business was auto safety and to the media who talked up the wisdom of seat belt use and demonstrated graphically through dramatic pictures of car crashes the dangers of its neglect. And then the laws changed. And when seat belt use became mandatory, a lot of people who hadn't been using them but who think of themselves as law-abiding citizens began strapping themselves in. Gradually that became habitual for most people. Gradually the mores of the society shifted and it was no longer thought to be macho or cool *not* to wear seat belts; it was thought to be *stupid*. And not just stupid. Failure to wear seat belts took on a social stigma and people who failed to wear them began to be thought of as bad citizens.

What does this have to do with the prevention of violence? Well, one of the reasons national leaders have so frequently used violence, especially against their own people, is because they could get away with it. It is one of the great myths of our time that much of the bloodshed of the past decade or two has been the result of long-standing ethnic and tribal tensions. It is true that those tensions have existed in places like Rwanda and Bosnia and Darfur, but in each case the different groups managed for decades to live together in relative harmony until one or more political leaders sought to exploit those underlying tensions for their own purposes and thought they would pay no price for their treachery.

One of the most promising developments of the modern era is that international law and institutions have evolved to a point where impunity like that is no longer inevitable. It started with the war crimes tribunals for Rwanda and the former Yugoslavia and traces its way through the 1999 decision of the British Law Lords that sovereign immunity did not protect Augusto Pinochet from prosecution for crimes against humanity. Indeed, when it comes to crimes like torture and genocide, any country on earth has the power to prosecute those responsible—it's called "universal jurisdiction"—if it can get its hands on them. And of course this promising arc now includes the International Criminal Court (the ICC), which has already issued indictments against alleged criminals in the Congo, Uganda, and Sudan, including now the president of Sudan who has, among many other things, sheltered Ahmed Haroun, one of the principal architects of the slaughter in Darfur, appointing him secretary of state for humanitarian affairs and hence cynically giving him oversight of the very people he is killing.

We have a long way to go before international jurisprudence will be a reliable resource for deterring violence—and of course the United States' own recalcitrance is a major stumbling block—but we are farther down this path today than I had any reason to hope we might be when I took up my work with Amnesty in 1994. And if the ICC is successful in its early prosecutions, imagine how much easier it will be to make the case to the American people that ratifying the Court's statutes, such that future Saddam Husseins could be dealt with judicially rather than militarily, is clearly and convincingly in America's best interests. With the *effective* criminalization of human rights crimes, we advance the notion at the global level that you *can* legislate morality and that eventually the norms of a civilized world will preclude torture and mass atrocities (and, not incidentally, mandate the shunning of those who commit them), just as they already do piracy and slavery.

But mention of Hussein brings us, of course, to the heart of the question before us: Until the day comes that no tyrant can assume impunity, how does the international community, within the constraints provided by our religious and ethical traditions, use its power to prevent or stop or punish grievous crimes against humanity? Ought we to reject the use of any and all kinds of violence and war to resolve disputes between peoples and nations and adopt a principle of seeking just peace through nonviolent means, as the pacifist tradition would aver? In part our answer will turn on what we believe the role of religious values and institutions to be. Should they hold up ideals in order to advance the highly honorable tradition of speaking truth to power, even when those ideals have little practical chance of being adopted and power cannot hear? Or should they sully their hands with the hard choices of policymaking, knowing that they may thereby compromise their claims to unblemished moral authority? If your answer is the former, there is really little more to say. But if your answer is the latter, as it has always been within most Western moral and religious traditions, the matter becomes far more complicated and interesting.

Of all the tragic aspects of the neoconservative movement over the past six or seven years, perhaps the greatest is that America's arrogance, adventurism, and exceptionalism (the sense that we make the rules and so we can break them at will) have made it far more difficult for us to provide leadership to the world—*moral or military*—even when doing so is in the best interest of a suffering humanity. I refer today to Darfur. A NATO-supplied no-fly zone over Darfur would have a very good chance of retarding, if not stopping, the genocide there dead in its tracks because the *janjaweed* militia would hesitate to operate without the cover of the Sudanese Air Force. But the moral authority of the United States is so compromised by Iraq and our capacity so overextended both there and in Afghanistan; the United States's intentions regarding the Muslim world are so suspect; and the American public is so wary of further military commitments, that we have allowed 250,000 people to die and 2.5 million to be displaced in Darfur without lifting a single weapon against its militia.

I admit that my view is colored here by my experience of Rwanda. The 1994 genocide in Rwanda took place two months after I had assumed the leadership of Amnesty, and I will forever be haunted by our inability to do more to stop it. Especially tormenting is how little force would have been required. General Romeo Dallaire, the Canadian general who was in charge of UN troops in Rwanda when the killing began—who subsequently suffered a breakdown over his failure to save lives, and who is one of the great unsung heroes of my generation—believed that it would have taken no more than fifteen hundred soldiers to save the lives of close to a million people. Fifteen hundred soldiers to save a million! If you doubt for a moment that the Rwandan genocide falls into the category of crimes that legitimize outside intervention, just reflect on the following confession from a man named Francois, held at Central Prison in the Rwandan capital of Kigali, for his part in the atrocities, and imagine similar situations being repeated tens of thousands of times:

> A car drove by with a loudspeaker saying that all Hutus had to defend themselves, that there was a single enemy: the Tutsis. I heard that. I jumped out of bed, grabbed a club, I went out, and I began killing. There was an old woman nearby, with two young children who had not reached school age yet. We took them outside and made them stand by a pit. . . . I killed the children and [a man named Sibomana] killed the old woman. Then we climbed back out [of the pit] and found an old man hiding behind the house. I knocked him out with a club. . . . I did not know the people I killed very well. All we were told was to hunt down the Tutsis, and we began to slaughter them. . . . While I was killing, I thought there was no problem, no consequences, since the authorities

said the Tutsis were enemies. My neighbors were Tutsis, we used to share everything like water. There weren't any conflicts between us. I don't know why all those things happened. Wickedness was in fashion.[2]

When wickedness is in fashion, it is sometimes simply impossible to do what a pacifist ideal asserts—namely, to secure a just peace through nonviolent means—because justice and peace often share separate bedchambers.

But how do we know that wickedness is truly in fashion and not just the whim of some maniacal fashion designer? Fortunately, just as international justice has evolved over the past years, so has the concept of the "responsibility to protect"—it has evolved to the point where the United Nations in 2003 adopted guidelines regarding when humanitarian military intervention is justified. It must, for example, be designed to counter large-scale loss of life or ethnic cleansing; it must be a last resort; it must receive some type of international imprimatur. Had these guidelines been followed, the United States would never have invaded Iraq in the first place, but we certainly would be taking far more proactive steps to stop the slaughter in Darfur.

So where does this leave us with regard to the choice between violence and nonviolence? It leaves us with a *no* when it comes to renouncing absolutely the use of force, but it leaves us with a loud and unqualified *yes* about all that we can do to curtail violence and limit the uses of force in international affairs. One of those things we can do is theological.

We are all tempted, in the face of our own failings, to lash out at others. But from a religious perspective, the appropriate response to a recognition of our own demons is not to demonize others. It is to seek out common bonds. It is to recognize that virtually all people, of whatever stripe, feel the need to be safe in their homes, to be treated fairly by the authorities, to pass on a better life to their children, and to enjoy their rightful share of the earth's abundance. Part of the job of a government is to make it as easy as possible for its citizens to be their best selves, not their ugliest and most degraded, and part of religion's job is to help us understand what those best selves look like. Let us not allow the stubborn, wrongheaded, pinched-nosed vision of neoconservatism to distract us from the fundamental recognition that we truly are our brothers' and sisters' keepers and that on rare occasions that fidelity requires us, with caution and humility to be sure, to dirty our hands in order to stay the worst monsters of the human heart's recesses.

William F. Schulz, a Senior Fellow at the Center for American Progress, served as Executive Director of Amnesty International USA from 1994 to 2006. An ordained minister, Dr. Schulz was president of the Unitarian Universalist Association of Congregations from 1985 to 1993.

Acknowledgments

In the late 1990s, retired ambassador Jonathan Dean spoke to a crowded auditorium at the University of Missouri–Columbia about the work of Global Action to Prevent War. His proposal for a phased program to prevent war, genocide, and internal armed conflict was persuasive to people across the political spectrum. He addressed our hopes for peace, our aversion to war, and our commitment to respond to crimes against humanity and armed aggression with foresight and creativity.

This book is a tribute to the work of Global Action to Prevent War (GAPW), and to other organizations committed to providing constructive alternatives to war. My understanding of the possibilities for enduring security and sustainable peace has been forged through my work with Saul Mendlovitz, Jonathan Dean, and the late Randall Forsberg. This work would not be possible without their astute analysis and sustained leadership in creating an international coalition of activists, nongovernmental organizations, and peace studies programs. This book is also inspired by the work of other members of GAPW, and I thank them for their support and encouragement: Robert Zuber, Lester Ruiz, Waverly de Bruijn,

Jennifer Nordstrom, Bill Wickersham, Robin Remington, Paul Wallace, Peter Linsenmeyer, Suzanne Burgoyne, Earl Lubensky, Lewis and Dolores Mead, Gladys Swan, Steve Starr, Betty Acree, and the late Margot Lubensky. I am also thankful for the support of the Center for the Arts and Humanities at the University of Missouri. With the leadership of Elaine Lawless, we convened a study group on understandings of security and peace that addressed the concerns and hopes of people who were conservative, liberal, and progressive. I learned much from Rev. Kim Ryan, Sarah Read, and Mary Barile about the possibilities for critical engagement with those of widely divergent political views. Both the possibility and necessity of critical dialogue across political lines were affirmed by my work with the Ford-funded Difficult Dialogues Project at the University of Missouri. We provided training for faculty in helping students address contentious political issues, moving beyond polarized positions and discovering areas of mutual concern and possible shared actions. I am deeply grateful to the other members of the research team: Roger Worthington, Noor Azizan-Gardner, Paul Ladehof, Suzanne Burgoyne, Sandra Hodges, Patricia Beckman, Antwaun Smith, Ed Lambeth, Robert Baum, Rachel Jones, Taleb Khairallah, Peggy Placier, and Lisa Flores.

In 2006 the Unitarian Universalist Association adopted the issue of peacemaking for a four-year period of study and reflection. I became a member of the core team coordinating this study process, and many of the insights found in this book emerged out of conversations with other members of that team: Judy Morgan, John Hooper, Adam Gerhardstein, Barbara Bates, Alex Winnet, Jim Nelson, Charlie Clements, Janice Marie Johnson, Larry Schafer, LoraKim Joyner, Rev. Frank Carpenter, Denny Davidson, and Mac Goekler. To them I offer my heartfelt thanks and gratitude.

I am also indebted to friends who have long pondered with me the ironies, absurdities, and satisfactions of sustained political engagement: Karen Touzeau, William Schulz, Mary McClintock Fulkerson, Carol Lee Sanchez, Amy Shapiro, Gary Oxenhandler, Bernie Beitman, Meg Riley, and Elaine Lawless. Their honesty, audacity, and generosity have profoundly shaped the way I see the world.

I am deeply thankful to my editor at Fortress Press, Michael West. Michael not only suggested the idea of this short book on peacebuilding, but provided encouragement and critical evaluation along the way. I am equally grateful to Pam Rumancik, Joe Cherry, and Scott Rudolph for providing a critical reading of the final manuscript. And, finally, thanks as well to my family, whose companionship and support are an ongoing source of inspiration and joy: my husband, Jon Poses; my daughters, Zoe and Hannah Welch; my brother and sister, Mark Welch and Rhonda Neighbour; and my indomitable grandmother, Edith Graef.

Sections of this book have appeared elsewhere in different forms. I would like to thank the publishers for permission to make use of the following materials:

Portions of "Politics after Empire: Dangerous Memories, Cultivated Awareness and Enlivening Engagement," in *Athens and Jerusalem on the Polis* (conference proceedings, Villanova University, October 27, 2006, edited by James Wetzel), are revised and incorporated into chapter 4.

Portions of "Artisans of Hope, Artisans of Wonder," in *Theology That Matters*, edited by Darby Kathleen Ray (Minneapolis: Fortress Press, 2006), 189–98, are revised and incorporated into the introduction and chapter 1.

Portions of chapter 6 of *After Empire: The Art and Ethos of Enduring Peace* (Minneapolis: Fortress Press, 2004) are revised and incorporated into chapter 4.

Introduction

Third-Wave Politics: Aesthetic Pragmatism and the Politics of Hope

In a world fraught with violence, what are realistic possibilities for enduring security and sustainable peace? I have been a lifelong member of groups working for peace, trying to find ways both to prevent war and to resolve conflict without violence. The horrors that William Schulz describes so clearly, the unspeakable cruelty of genocide and the brutality of domination, have been our world. If not immediate victims of war and displacement ourselves, we are aware of such cruelty as the horizon of our responsibility and our concern. The question that Schulz poses so clearly is also our question—the focus of our political analysis, our theological and ethical reflections, and our activism as citizens of particular countries and as citizens of the world: "How does the international community, within the constraints provided by our religious and ethical traditions, use its power to prevent or stop or punish grievous crimes against humanity?" I invite you to join us in an exploration of this question—of political challenges and opportunities, of traditions that may well constrain, as Schulz states, our baser impulses, as well as traditions that may evoke our more compassionate and creative selves.

There is no doubt that this work is serious—it is, quite literally, a matter of life and death. We know the devastating cost of unchecked crimes against humanity: in Darfur there have been thousands of women and girls raped, 250,000 people killed, and 2.5 million displaced. We know as well the horrendous toll of waging war. By August 2008, well over four thousand U.S. troops had died, and the number of those grievously injured was approaching fourteen thousand. Estimates of the numbers of Iraqi civilians and soldiers killed since the U.S. invasion of 2003 range from 151,000 to over a million.[1]

Are we caught in a struggle between two equally devastating choices: engage in either the hazards and brutality of war or stand by while millions are displaced and thousands killed? Although the choices may seem grim, there are other options. There are ways of responding that allow us to act decisively to protect civilians from genocide and crimes against humanity but do not take us into the spiral of all-out war, with its devastating toll on civilians and military forces alike. To find an effective third way between waging war and doing nothing is not easy. There is no doubt that it requires the best of us—our most astute planning, our open hearts, and creative institution building. It also requires patience, persistence, and a recognition of the simple fact that the task of preventing and responding to grave forms of injustice is not an aberration, an interruption of our work as human beings, but simply an ongoing part of what it means to exist as creatures who have immense powers of cruelty as well as immense capacities for generosity and empathy.

In these pages I will tell a story—one of the multiple forms of creativity that graces our world—of the many ways in which people throughout the world and across the political spectrum are finding fitting and resonant ways of building enduring security and sustainable peace. I will describe the political initiatives that are being taken and the ethical and theological questions that they pose. I will also examine the implications of these initiatives, not just for building peace in particular, but for political activism in general.

Paradigm Shift

In an interview conducted in 1980, the French philosopher Michel Foucault gave a poetic invocation of social critique:

> I can't help but dream about a kind of criticism that would try not to judge but to bring an oeuvre, a book, a sentence, an idea to life; it would light fires, watch the grass grow, listen to the wind, and catch the sea foam in the breeze and scatter it. It would multiply not judgments but signs of existence; it would summon them, drag them from their sleep. Perhaps it would invent them sometimes—all the better. All the better. Criticism that hands down sentences sends me to sleep; I'd like a criticism of scintillating leaps of the imagination. It would not be sovereign or dressed in red. It would bear the lightning of possible storms.[2]

Foucault's dream is our reality. We are in the midst of a third wave of revolutionary politics—one that builds on two prior waves and yet has its own energy, dynamics, and challenges.

The first wave of revolutionary politics was the forceful denunciation of manifold forms of social injustice—slavery, the oppression of workers, and the secondary status of women—all forms of oppression defended for millennia as divinely ordained or part of the natural order of things.

In his book *Bury the Chains*, author Adam Hochschild reminds us of the audacity of the abolitionist movement. Within a century, an institution that had endured since the beginning of recorded human history lost its moral and political legitimacy. That the ongoing struggle against "natural" hierarchies would be neither easy nor inevitable was signaled, however, in the resistance of William Wilberforce (one of the leaders of the British abolitionist movement) to economic, political, or educational rights for the British working class.[3]

These struggles for social justice have been augmented by a second wave of activism, the work of identity politics, the resolute claim for the complex identities and full humanity of all groups marginalized and exploited by systemic oppression and silenced through cultural imperialism.

While the work for social justice and for the full recognition of human rights for all peoples goes on, these tasks now occur within a constructive framework. Once we recognize that a situation is unjust, once we grant the imperative of including the voices and experiences of all peoples, how then do we work together to build just and creative institutions?

This constructive work is taking place on many fronts. Before we explore two of the most notable—strategic peacebuilding and the development of community economies—a brief reflection on the shift from necessary reaction and critique to equally vital constructive political engagement is in order.

I was first aware that the task of governing well might be substantially different than that of denouncing and dismantling unjust social systems when I read the obituary of Joe Slovo in the *New York Times*. Joe Slovo was a longtime member of the African National Congress. In his obituary, he was cited as saying that nothing in his work in revolutionary politics had prepared him for the challenges of being minister of housing in the post-apartheid Mandela government. He was committed to adequate housing for all, had access to the resources to build such housing, and yet found that the challenges of equitably and efficiently accomplishing that task were daunting.[4]

Another story that led me to think more critically about the comforting narrative of "us against them on the road to certain victory" lies in the poignant contrast between the *Motorcycle Diaries* and the *Bolivian Diaries* of Che Guevara. The *Motorcycle Diaries* was profoundly moving in its heartfelt depiction of unjust suffering. The *Bolivian Diaries*, while written with as much honesty and as much compassion for the suffering of other human beings, was profoundly disturbing—marked by the despair and confusion of a hero of the Cuban revolution, disenchanted by his failures within the Cuban government as minister of industries and dispirited by his inability to find a mode of revolutionary action suitable for other countries. Although hunted, and ultimately executed, by the CIA and the Bolivian Army, he was also rejected by those he sought as allies—Bolivian communists who had their own view of the best means of radical social transformation in the Bolivian context. Still committed to justice, Che labored on, providing medical care for wounded Bolivian soldiers, yet feeling an outsider, unsure of how to work for justice in different situations, either as a member of government or as a revolutionary.[5]

And finally, on a very modest scale, a personal experience of the distinction between critique and constructive engagement: the lessons learned as director of women's studies. Seeing how hard it was for a group of well-intentioned and politically astute radical feminists to run a degree program did give me pause. Maybe we weren't quite ready to take over the World Bank and other reins of institutional power.

Three different stories, yet a common thread. To care passionately about justice, to understand thoroughly the contours and dynamics of oppression, does not mean that we know how to cultivate and manage human and natural resources justly, creatively, and in a way that lasts for the future.

Third-Wave Political Engagement

Although it is undoubtedly difficult to live justly, to use power truthfully and well, it is not impossible to do so. Let us turn to two such examples of third-wave political engagement: strategic peacebuilding and community economies.

J. K. Gibson-Graham (Katherine Gibson, Australian National University in Canberra, and Julie Graham, University of Massachusetts–Amherst, writing as a single persona since 1992) describe a new political imaginary. They analyze, nurture, and celebrate the reality, opportunities, and challenges of community economies. People all over the world are finding ways of shaping their economic lives to recognize the power of interdependence, not a "common being" but a "being in common." J. K. Gibson-Graham describe "employee buyouts in the United States, worker takeovers in the wake of economic crisis in Argentina, the anti-sweatshop movement, shareholder movements that promote ethical investments and police the enforcement of corporate

environmental and social responsibly, the living wage
movement, discussions of a universal basic income,
social entrepreneurship—all part of a community economy that performs economy in new ways."[6]

Gibson-Graham build on the insights of queer theory,
political and feminist theory, and organizing, emphasiz-
ing that shared questions often lead to different answers.
Just as there is not one way to be a feminist, there is no
single way to perform economic relations justly. There
are, however, salient questions, choices to be made in
each situation. Here the economy becomes the product
of ethical decision making, different ways of answering
the same questions:

- what is *necessary* to personal and social survival;
- how social *surplus* is appropriated and distributed;
- whether and how social surplus is to be produced
  and *consumed*; and
- how a *commons* is produced and sustained.[7]

In making these choices, J. K. Gibson-Graham make
a claim as startling as that of there being no preferred
model of economic justice: it is as difficult for workers
to live within community economies as it is for owners.
For all of us, the challenge of new forms of subjectivity, sociality, and interdependence are "best shaped by
practical curiosity as opposed to moral certainty about
alternatives to capitalism."[8]

Let us turn to another example of third-wave political activism, the current options for attaining enduring
human security and sustainable, participatory peace.
When I was first a peace activist, the choices facing
us were clear: the limited violence of just war or the
renunciation of violence in any form. Now, however,
our options are greater and our choices more complex.

Since the early 1990s, the world of peace activism and peace studies has been transformed by a focus on the vast areas of concern shared by proponents of nonviolence and by supporters of just war. The debate between advocates of just war and advocates of pacifism is being transformed and augmented by a *third way*: joint efforts to prevent war, stop genocide, and repair the damage caused by armed conflict. Activists and scholars such as Glenn Stassen and Lisa Schirch are asking a new set of questions: If war is the last resort, what are the first, second, third, fourth, and fifth responses to aggression, domination, and exploitation? And if war is not the answer, what is the answer to structural violence and terrorism? How can armed conflicts be prevented? How can the deep wounds of war-ravaged societies be healed?[9]

We live in a time of three constructive approaches to peace: (1) peacekeeping—early intervention to stop genocide and prevent large-scale war, (2) peacemaking—bringing hostile parties to agreement, and (3) peacebuilding—the creation of long-term structures for redressing injustice and resolving ongoing conflict. Many of us know well the work of peacebuilding—addressing the root causes of armed conflict, economic exploitation, and political marginalization. We also are becoming more aware of what is involved in the complex work of peacemaking—negotiating equitable and sustainable peace agreements, ones that include attention to the pressing need for post-conflict restoration and reconciliation. Not so many people, however, are aware of current developments in peacekeeping.

While United Nations peacekeeping operations have been formed on a case-by-case basis, this ad hoc response to genocide and armed conflict is increasingly seen as unsatisfactory, as is now the case, tragically and unnecessarily, in Darfur. As Kofi Annan states, "The United Nations is the only fire prevention agency that has to establish a fire department after the fire has broken out."[10] There are, therefore, ongoing efforts to establish standing nonviolent conflict resolution centers and permanent peacekeeping forces both at the United Nations and within regional cooperation and security organizations. For example, organizing efforts—like those that led to the creation of the International Criminal Court—have begun for the creation of a standing United Nations Emergency Peace Service. Such a service would be constituted by up to fifteen thousand volunteers, medical personnel, lawyers, judges, engineers, construction personnel, and trained peacekeepers, and would be capable of being deployed within forty-eight hours in a crisis situation.[11]

The mandate of peacekeeping forces, while certainly important, is nonetheless limited. Peacekeeping forces do not have the objective of defeating an enemy but have, rather, the complex task of clearing the space where negotiations can either resume or begin. Such interventions are more like community policing than military campaigns, requiring careful coordination with civil society, and aim to restore a society's internal sense of order.

These three tasks—peacemaking, peacebuilding, and peacekeeping—are all needed to bring about enduring security and sustainable peace. Each is an integral part of successful United Nations peace operations. Each is essential in what many peace activists call *strategic peacebuilding*.[12]

Despite the promise of strategic peacebuilding as an alternative to military intervention, it, too, has constitutive risks and dangers. While the sole reliance on military force is undoubtedly destructive and counter-productive, strategic peacebuilding may also have unintended negative consequences. Lisa Schirch, professor of peacebuilding at Eastern Mennonite University's Center for Justice and Peacebuilding, describes the salient risks and dangers of strategic peacebuilding: "Peacebuilding programs do not always contribute to peace." Not only are there technical challenges in coordinating short-term and long-term efforts, but all of the tasks of intervention are complicated by "ideological differences, ego-driven efforts to monopolize peacebuilding programs, and competitions for resources."[13] Catherine Barnes, drawing on her analysis of global peacemaking efforts, affirms Schirch's critique. She also points to the destructive effects of tensions between the goals of external agencies and the aspirations and expertise of local people and groups. Furthermore, Barnes claims that the work of both "insiders and outsiders" falters when they "involve only those predisposed to peace" and fail to include in some meaningful way "those who instigate" or support violence.[14]

Surely there is one place, however, where nonviolence is an unalloyed good: nonviolent campaigns to challenge structural violence and injustice.

In 1963, in Birmingham, Alabama, the resolute claim that separate but equal was justified, that segregation was a just form of social order, was shown to be a lie by the brutal attacks of white police officers on marching children and young people. The sit-in campaigns across the South served to unmask the civility of segregation when they ended in vicious attacks by white people on those attempting to integrate buses and lunch counters.

Nonviolent direct action can undoubtedly be an extremely effective means of exposing injustice. There are, however, intrinsic dangers in such action. First, a specific form of direct action, powerful in some instances, can become rote and ineffective through overuse. Mass marches often have tremendous impact on those who participate in them, serving the inspiring and unifying function of the church services that regularly preceded the marches of the civil rights movement. They do not, however, communicate effectively with those who oppose their message.

Second, as Lisa Schirch reminds us, nonviolent direct action is a form of coercion that cannot build peace alone: nonviolent direct action "escalates conflict and can often temporarily increase antagonism and tensions between people and groups." While the peace disrupted by direct action is itself faulty and incomplete, nonviolent direct action may further disrupt community bonds. The coercion of direct action needs, therefore, to be followed by the work of reconciliation and restoration.[15] Mahatma Gandhi and Martin Luther King Jr. knew this well. Gandhi refused to vilify the British while condemning British rule, holding firmly to nonviolence of thought, word, and deed. King also appealed to the sense of justice of white Americans, calling all races to a place in the "beloved community."[16]

How can we do for our time what Gandhi and King did with such courage and creativity for theirs? Let us honor the nonviolent movements of the past in the aesthetic register of jazz—not by simply repeating their strategies, but by finding ones that call our communities to fuller participation in the beloved community.

To participate in the beloved community with honesty and integrity demands of us that we face, without excuses, the ways in which our social order falls short of our cherished ideals. It also requires that we examine the ways in which the stories we tell ourselves—the stories of who we are, what we have suffered, and what we have achieved—may hinder the work of healing and reconciliation.

In his study of identity-based conflicts in South Africa, Eastern Europe, and Canada, Vern Redekop points to what is essential for healing and reconciliation: ways of framing collective and individual identity that provide a deep sense of the past (incorporating "memory, story and coherence") and an equally evocative sense of the future (rich with "imagination, stimulation and continuity"). The problem, however, is that such collective stories are often self-righteous and self-justifying narratives of exclusion, framing the past and the future in terms of "us against them," either innocent victims bravely resisting a demonic foe, or beneficent victors proudly bearing all humanity's destiny. How do we convey other stories, ones of blessing and abundance, vitality and honest self-critique?[17]

In these reflections on the challenges of strategic peacebuilding we find a compelling story: a firm commitment to constructive peacebuilding and the prevention of armed conflict, yet a sober recognition of the limits of peacebuilding and the fallibility of peacebuilders, peacemakers, and peacekeepers.

Let us step back for a moment. What does the work of building community economies have to do with the challenges of peacebuilding? In both forms of transformative activism we find an enlivening critique of injustice that, to use Foucault's words, "multiplies signs of existence." And, equally important, the critique of external forces and structures is matched by the awareness of our own limits, errors, and failures of creativity and connection.

How do we hold together these threads of insight and courage, external violence and internal limitations, in our work for social justice? How might we view our task if we see the ways in which our internal conflicts and lack of imagination may play a role in our political failures? How do we maintain presence, creativity, *and* openness to our own responsibility and fallibility? Let me first tell you a story, source unknown, that I have heard as long as I have been an activist.

A man comes to a city and is outraged by the injustice he sees. He stands in the center of the town square and demands justice. At first a large crowd gathers, but each day, it dwindles until he stands alone—a solitary voice denouncing the evil that continues unabated. One day a passerby asks him, "Why do you speak in the square each day since you are not changing anyone?" His answer: "At first I spoke to change others; now I speak so that they will not change me."

Where can we find another story, one that has the honesty to admit that our failures to change others may well be of our own making—not necessarily the lack of insight, courage, and compassion in others, but a lack of creativity, skill, and empathy in ourselves? In this book we will engage in such a story, an examination of the contours of peacekeeping, peacemaking, and peacebuilding with regard to the dilemmas and opportunities that are ours.

My own work in this area, both as an activist and as a scholar, is profoundly shaped by my life growing up on a ranch in West Texas and the ethos that surrounded us in that world. It was an ethos of responding to the vagaries of human life—whether dust storms, hard freezes, or shifting global markets and farm policies—with an audacious yet grounded pragmatic creativity. We worked together to bring as much justice as possible, to grow as fine a crop as feasible, within the constraints and with the resources at hand. I continue to learn from this world and have realized that there is a continuing convergence between the challenges of ranching and work for justice. In a recent conversation with my cousin Brent Graef, Brent stated that when he first began training horses, his goal was to make the wrong thing difficult. Now his goal has changed. He finds himself working horses in a way that makes the right thing obvious.

What is the right thing in regard to genocide, to structural injustice, to violent conflicts between and within states? In the pages that follow, we will find answers that are evocative but not definitive—strategies that emerge from an aesthetic pragmatism, a way of responding to the limits and possibilities of the present with honesty, audacity, courage, and compassion.

1

Peacekeeping

Achieving and sustaining national and international security has never been easy. Our time is hardly unique in the range and magnitude of threats to economic and political stability. Like generations before us, we face the challenges of responding to massive violations of human rights by leaders who are unable, or unwilling, to protect their own populations from genocide. We face the dilemmas of dealing with dictators who are unaccountable to their own people, undeterred by international public opinion, and defended by powerful allies. We confront conflicts within and between nations in which fragile peace agreements are all too easily derailed by spoilers, parties more interested in the gains of war than the promises of peace.

We see in our daily press and news media the stories of grievous pain, harm, and unnecessary suffering. We know, too, the slow pace of response. Despite the heartfelt determination "never again" to allow genocide to go unstopped, the response to the devastation in Darfur has been painfully cumbersome, more a response of heartfelt outrage than effective intervention. And the tragic events in Darfur are not unique: women and girls raped, thousands displaced from their homes, and a government either unwilling or unable to stop the assaults. Such grave crimes against humanity have happened before and are likely to happen again. In our world, serious threats to security are not just posed by conflicts between states. Rather, we are facing, and will likely continue to face, dire threats to human security caused by national disasters, intranational conflicts, and governmental repression.

These problems demand the best of us all as citizens of an international community, our hearts touched by suffering so far away, and well aware that our own security and national interest are imperiled by insecurity throughout the world.[1]

In addition, however, to these reports of grave suffering and of cumbersome and inadequate response, there is another unfolding story. Throughout the world, individuals, organizations, and governments are exploring long-lasting, effective ways of responding to crimes against humanity and threats to human security. These efforts are multidimensional and draw on the decades of experience—mistakes and failures as well as successes—of United Nations peace operations and international peacemaking endeavors since the end of World War II. These efforts are vast and they are beginning to be more closely integrated and well funded. This is the story of strategic peacebuilding—a global enterprise to build enduring security and sustainable peace. There are three components of strategic peacebuilding: peacekeeping, peacemaking, and peacebuilding. We will examine each of them in turn, beginning with peacekeeping—the use of multilateral armed forces to prevent large-scale war and to stop genocide and crimes against humanity.

I will introduce you to some of the central organizations and people shaping this creative response to human security. The actors are as varied as the tasks are complex. This is an enterprise that involves people across the political spectrum—conservatives, liberals, and progressives. It is a third way of working for international and national security, a development that is building on the strengths and learning from the weaknesses of both principled nonviolence and just war traditions.

Evolution of United Nations Peacekeeping Operations

Peacekeeping is the beginning of a long process aimed at attaining sustainable peace. It is not an end in itself.[2]

Since 1945, three generations of peacekeeping operations have been conducted by the United Nations. Over the decades, there have been significant shifts in the mandate given to peacekeeping missions and a mixed record of success and failure. People within the UN, as well as people outside the organization, have analyzed UN peacekeeping operations. In 1995, then Secretary General Kofi Annan formed the Lessons Learned Unit, and in 2006, political scientists Michael Doyle and Nicholas Sambanis published *Making War and Building Peace*, a comprehensive analysis of three generations of peacekeeping operations. Both studies reached similar conclusions: a basic recognition of the "multidimensional nature" of peacekeeping and the need to integrate "military, political, humanitarian, and human rights elements."[3]

This understanding of the need for long-term and multidimensional work has only emerged gradually, as the task of peacekeeping has evolved. Doyle and Sambanis describe the differences between three generations of UN peacekeeping operations. First-generation peacekeeping operations were formed in response to conflicts between states. In 1948, the first secretary general of the United Nations, Trygve Lie, argued for the creation of a small United Nations force to deal with the violence in Jerusalem. He thought that such forces should have a mandate that included the use of armed force, not only in self-defense, but also in defense of civilian populations. Political circumstances, however, led to a different focus: multilateral forces whose function was primarily that of monitoring, rather than enforcing, cease-fires and peace agreements. In these operations, the UN sought the consent of all parties to the conflict. The first such peacekeeping operation was in 1956, the separation of Israel and Egypt following the French, British, and Israeli intervention in Suez.[4] Not only did these forces intervene with the consent of the parties to the conflict, but their mandate was strictly limited: force would not be used, except in self-defense, and they were not responsible for meeting humanitarian needs (delivery of basic resources, protection from unjust authorities, and so on).[5]

Second-generation peacekeeping operations were also based on consent but had a larger goal—that of actively pursuing the implementation of peace agreements. This led to a large array of tasks, all designed to lay the foundation for sustainable peace and enduring security. In addition to monitoring peace agreements, these forces took on a more active role in post-civil-war situations. United Nations peacekeepers were asked to monitor cease-fires; rebuild devastated economies; support the reform of key institutions such as the police, army, and judicial systems; implement fair elections; disarm hostile parties; and assist in the safe return of refugees. Doyle and Sambanis claim that these efforts have been substantially successful in a number of cases of civil war, such as Namibia, El Salvador, Cambodia, Mozambique, and Eastern Slavonia.[6]

Third-generation peacekeeping operations incorporate the previously mentioned tasks but do not have the assent of all parties to a conflict. Without such assent, they become "peace-enforcing" operations that are more similar to military interventions than the prior two types of operations. These interventions take a number of forms, from using armed forces to enable the delivery of humanitarian aid, to enforcing cease-fires, maintaining no-fly zones, or enforcing the implementation of peace agreements. Third-generation peacekeeping operations are only successful when the forces have enough military strength and enough popular support to impose terms on recalcitrant parties. In these operations, force is used in self-defense and is also used to support the mandate as a whole. While at times successful, third-generation peacekeeping faces the same dangers of any type of imperialist intervention: significant resistance from the host government and local population.[7]

Third-generation peacekeeping operations are designed to respond to the failures of first- and second-generation peacekeeping operations to stop genocide. In Rwanda, eight hundred thousand people were killed, as General Dallaire was unable to get permission to allow UN troops to protect civilians. Without a mandate to use force, UN troops also stood by as eight thousand Bosnian men in the Srebrenica region of Bosnia-Herzegovina were killed.[8] Many people within the United Nations and throughout the world have vowed never again to allow such passivity in the face of massive violence.

Third-generation peacekeeping operations face, however, another dilemma: the failure of force to stop crimes against humanity. In Somalia, for example, local forces resisted U.S. forces and UN forces alike. The scene of the bodies of U.S. servicemen being paraded through the streets of Mogadishu led many people in the U.S. to reject such interventions as a foolhardy exercise and a tragic waste of human life, paving the way for deadly inaction in Rwanda and Bosnia.[9] And the 1999 NATO bombing campaign in Kosovo, while possibly saving lives, remains controversial because of the lack of Security Council approval and the dangerous precedent of illegal interventions in the affairs of a sovereign state.[10]

Leonard Kapungu describes the gist of the dilemma now facing the international community:

> By 1995, a number of significant . . . developments coalesced to convince UN senior officials that something had gone terribly wrong with UN peacekeeping. . . . These included the horrific ethnic cleansing that occurred in the former Yugoslavia [in the early 1990s], in the presence of the United Nations Protective Force. . . ; the terrifying genocide in Rwanda in 1994 as the bulk of the forces of the United Nations Mission in Rwanda . . . withdrew; and an unfulfilled mandate in Somalia following the withdrawal of the United Nations Operation in Somalia.[11]

Given these striking failures, some propose that third-generation operations be delegated to regional organizations with more military strength, such as NATO. Whether these operations are delegated to others, however, or carried by the UN, the core issues are the same: When is peacekeeping warranted? What needs can it meet with a relative likelihood of success? How do we maintain a clear distinction between peacekeeping and waging war? And once we have an international commitment to protect peoples from genocide and crimes against humanity, what institutional capabilities are required to act on this commitment?

In answering these questions, governmental leaders and concerned citizens face an interlocking set of problems—responses that are ad hoc rather than carefully planned and coordinated, and responses that lack a clear international consensus regarding either the conditions for international intervention or the best means of intervening.

Under the leadership of Kofi Annan, the international community began to address this complex set of issues:

> When a government cannot or will not protect its citizens from rape, mass murder, and other crimes against humanity, does the international community have the responsibility to protect those peoples from ongoing catastrophe? Within many circles of the international community, the answer is increasingly a resounding "yes."[12]

In addition to a widespread recognition of the need for an international response to crimes against humanity, there is an equally pervasive recognition of the significant dangers in a too-easy rush to humanitarian intervention. Such interventions may well serve as a mask for neocolonial intervention. In order to examine these dual concerns—an equal sense of the imperative and the danger of multilateral humanitarian intervention—the Canadian government established the International Commission on Intervention and State Sovereignty in September 2000. The Commission was comprised of twelve members from Australia, Algeria, Canada, the United States, Russia, Germany, South Africa, the Philippines, Switzerland, Guatemala, and India. The members were Gareth Evans and Mohamed Sahnoun, cochairs, and Gisele Cote-Harper, Lee Hamilton, Michael Ignatieff, Vladimir Lukin, Klaus Naumann, Cyril Ramaphosa, Fidel Ramos, Cornelio Sommaruga, Eduardo Stein, and Ramesh Thakur.[13]

The Commission published its findings, *The Responsibility to Protect*, in December 2001. In this document we find a compelling articulation of an emerging political consensus about the responsibility of states to protect their citizens from mass murder, systematic rape, and other crimes against humanity—and the responsibility of the international community to intervene when they do not. The ground of the consensus was clear: "We want no more Rwandas." The content of the consensus, however, was complex: given the obligation to protect citizens from ethnic cleansing and genocide, the question remains of authority and implementation: Who decides when intervention is warranted? What are the best means of stopping ethnic cleansing and other crimes against humanity? What are the dangers in even multilateral intervention, and how are they best checked?[14]

The members of the Commission explored these questions in a series of steps. They first described an emerging sense of global citizenship and global danger. The tragedy of Rwanda was not an aberration. Throughout the world we find other internal conflicts in which civilian populations are the direct target of systemic rape, deliberate displacement, and mass murder.[15]

In the face of these all-too-common threats, the Commission proposed two criteria for the use of military force by the international community:

In the Commission's view, military intervention for human protection purposes is justified in two broad sets of circumstances, namely in order to halt or avert:

- *large scale loss of life, actual or apprehended, with genocidal intent or not, which is the product either of deliberate state action, or state neglect or inability to act, or a failed state situation; or*

- *large scale "ethnic cleansing," actual or apprehended, whether carried out by killing, forced expulsion, acts of terror or rape.*[16]

These criteria encompass the devastation of ethnic cleansing and the large-scale loss of life and mass starvation, whether caused by deliberate acts, state collapse, or natural disasters. While the criteria are clear, making the decision to intervene is never simple, never uncontested. As in the case of Darfur, while there is widespread international agreement that there are grave crimes against humanity, the government itself denies that genocide is taking place. It is here that impartial agencies such as Amnesty International and Human Rights Watch have an essential role to play in assessing the type and degree of violations of human rights and the extent of the threats to survival and well-being.[17]

In determining when military intervention is necessary, the Commission also described the types of injustice that warrant sustained action but do not warrant military intervention without the consent of the government and other parties to the conflict. Widespread human rights violations, racial discrimination, imprisonment and repression of political opponents, and even the overthrow of a democratically elected government do not warrant military intervention by the UN or regional security forces, but are best met through internal political pressure, international diplomatic interventions, and economic and political sanctions. While these threats are certainly serious, deserving international attention and redress, intervention without consent is limited to cases of massive ethnic cleansing and loss of life.[18]

In cases of genocide and ethnic cleansing, the Commission provides a clear description of the moral and political reasons for international response. First, the moral imperative, described in uncompromising terms:

> Millions of human beings remain at the mercy of civil wars, insurgencies, state repression and state collapse. This is a stark and undeniable reality, and it is at the heart of all the issues with which this Commission has been wrestling. What is at stake here is not making the world safe for big powers, or trampling over the sovereign rights of small ones, but delivering practical protection for ordinary people, at risk of their lives, because their states are unwilling or unable to protect them.[19]

Refugees fleeing civil war, people dying at the hands of repressive governmental forces: these events, seemingly so far away, are not as removed as we might want to think. This is not simply a matter of compassionate outsiders responding to the needs of people at risk. No, there is another compelling reason for intervention. The Commission asserts a salient and compelling fact: we in the United States and Europe are often directly complicit in these tragic events. We provide the arms to the warring factions; our colonial partition of territories has led to unstable national configurations and ongoing conflicts over national identity and the control of natural resources.[20]

Not only are we a part of the problem, but these conflicts pose a security risk to all nations. The damage they cause is international in scope: the need to provide sanctuary and resources for refugees, the economic threat of destabilized markets and disrupted access to natural resources, and the possible spread of armed conflict into neighboring countries.[21]

Another reason for responding lies in the precedent that it sets for the model of good international citizenship. Sharing resources at one country's time of need may well mean that others are more likely to help when we ourselves face problems that we cannot solve alone: "There is much direct reciprocal benefit to be gained in an interdependent, globalized world where nobody can solve all their own problems: my country's assistance for you today in solving your neighborhood refugee and terrorism problem, might reasonably lead you to be more willing to help solve my environmental or drugs problem tomorrow."[22]

The strongest case for response is, of course, one shared most broadly: the moral imperative of saving the lives of other human beings. The Commission argues that "political leaders often underestimate the sheer sense of decency and compassion that prevails in their electorates . . . and the public willingness . . . to accept the risk of casualties in well designed military interventions aimed at alleviating that suffering."[23] We see evidence of such concern in the work of groups whose members resolutely pressure their governments not only to condemn genocide but also to act to prevent it. Globally, Amnesty International has an exemplary record of mobilizing support for those whose human rights are violated. In its Urgent Action campaigns, Amnesty has a success record of significantly improving the treatment of 40 percent of the cases in which people take direct action to express their outrage and concern over the violation of human rights.[24] And there is a proliferation of groups such as STAND, a student anti-genocide coalition, and Save Darfur, a coalition of 180 faith-based advocacy and humanitarian organizations, working to mobilize public support and political will for substantial intervention to stop the crimes against humanity in Darfur.[25]

Responses to Genocide and Crimes against Humanity

Once the decision is made that the international community must act, what are the best means of responding? While there may be willingness to act and a demand for action, as is now the case in Darfur, we lack standing peacekeeping forces, ready to be quickly deployed in a coherent, well-planned manner, and suitable to the situation at hand. While more than 150 heads of state at the UN Summit in 2005 affirmed the responsibility of the international community to protect people from crimes against humanity, they did not create the institutional means and procedures to respond to those crimes. We have, therefore, an "international norm" without corresponding international institutions. Here we confront the gap between commitment and capability.[26]

There is increasing international support for the establishment of standing, well-trained, multilateral peacekeeping forces. There is an equally strong consensus that peacekeeping forces must include far more than armed personnel and that the use of force by those personnel is most effective when it is clearly differentiated from the task of waging war. In the proposal for a United Nations Emergency Peace Service (UNEPS), for example, we find an emphasis on standing forces with a multifaceted mandate:

1. It will be a permanent standing force based at UN-designated sites.
2. It will be capable of rapid response, able to respond to an emergency within 48 hours.
3. It will be coherently organized under a unified UN command.
4. It will involve as many as 15,000 personnel, individually recruited from many different countries and demonstrating skills in conflict resolution, humanitarian assistance, law enforcement and other peacekeeping capabilities.
5. UNEPS personnel will receive comprehensive, expert training in peacekeeping with an emphasis on human rights and gender issues.
6. UNEPS will supplement existing UN and regional peacekeeping operations, providing another tool to support international efforts to end genocide and crimes against humanity.
7. UNEPS will be financed through the regular UN budget.[27]

The work of emergency peacekeeping forces may need to be followed by the longer-term deployment of peacekeeping forces, under the auspices of either the UN or regional security forces. In each case, however, the range of tasks is the same and reflects a paradigm shift in regard to security and the use of armed force. While force may well be necessary, it is never sufficient. Such operations are, therefore, significantly different from waging war, where the objective is to destroy the enemy's military capabilities. Here the goal is to protect human lives with as little force as possible.[28]

The Commission and the proponents of UNEPS claim that basic security and protection are best provided by a mixture of unarmed civilians and armed military personnel. Force is often needed to protect populations at the onset of a conflict, and after a conflict is resolved, force is often needed to stop revenge killings and retaliatory ethnic cleansing by those who were previously the victims of attack.[29]

Lisa Schirch describes the ways in which peacekeeping forces are like community policing efforts both in their mandate to restrain violence and in their need for self-restraint. For the past thirty years, cities throughout the United States and Europe have been moving away from traditional policing to community policing.[30] As Catherine Mullhaupt and Jean Hughes Raber state in their 2000 review, community policing leads police officers to become partners with the community in meeting basic needs for security and safety. Within this joint task, both members of civil society and of the police departments have a role. Police officers have a range of options, from "patting a young person on the back to the use of deadly force."[31]

Even in cases in which integrated peacekeeping operations may stop or prevent genocide and ethnic cleansing, far more work is required to establish enduring security and sustainable peace. Take, for example, the intervention in the Solomon Islands. In 2006, Oxfam published a study of the largely successful peacekeeping efforts by the Regional Assistance Mission to Solomon Islands (RAMSI), a deployment of police and military forces designed to address an armed conflict that had begun in 1998. Despite the improved security that resulted when fighting was stopped and militias were disarmed, Oxfam found that basic issues of economic and political inequality and of domestic violence remain unresolved. They found "a widespread lack of confidence that current proposals for economic development in Solomon Islands will benefit all." As the authors of the Oxfam report conclude, we do not yet have clearly coordinated means of integrating the work of peacemaking with simultaneous efforts at post-conflict reconstruction and peacebuilding. Successful peacekeeping efforts may stop armed violence yet fail to address deeper social and economic problems.[32]

Here we find a constitutive limit of even the most successful peacekeeping operations. They prepare the ground for further work to be done—that of peacemaking and peacebuilding—but cannot accomplish those tasks themselves. We will explore those tasks in the next chapter. Before we move to those two constructive tasks, however, let us examine some of the other constitutive dangers of peacekeeping operations and how they might be addressed.

Dangers of Humanitarian Intervention

One of the major problems in international peacekeeping has been a lack of consistent response. In his study of the case of Liberia and the need for "collective security" to sustain global order, law professor Ikechi Mgbeoji points to a discomfiting racial pattern: slow or nonexistent international response in the case of crimes against humanity that occur in Africa, and relatively quick action when European lives are at risk.

> In spite of clear, ample, and timely warnings by Canadian Major General Romeo Dallaire, the UN force commander in Rwanda, and a security operative of the Rwandan government that there was a looming

genocide of the Tutsis, powerful states on the Security Council, especially the United States under President Bill Clinton, stood by while "800,000 people were put to death in the most unambiguous case of state-sponsored genocide . . . since the Nazi Holocaust. . . . Similar indifference was seen in the case of Zaire, Sierra Leone, Madagascar. . . ."[33]

There are other causes of inconsistency. Even when the crimes are undeniable, the Commission noted that interventions may be blocked because of the resistance of other major powers, and therefore be politically impossible. Furthermore, when support is finally attained, it may be as much for reasons of national self-interest as for purely humanitarian concerns. Governments that decide to support intervention may do so to "avoid refugee outflows" or to prevent "a haven for drug producers or terrorists, developing in one's neighbourhood."[34]

Not only is the record of intervention inconsistent, but there is a widespread recognition that the claim of humanitarian intervention could be used as a mask for neocolonial domination, intervening more for the interest of the intervening state than to protect people at grave risk. Law professor Richard Falk makes this case strongly in his analysis of both the imperative and the danger of humanitarian intervention. Such interventions could easily become the vehicle for the domination and exploitation of weaker countries. The legacy of colonialism, exploitation under the guise of the beneficent spread of commerce and civilization, must not be ignored. And we are in danger of ignoring this history if we use what Falk calls the language of "self-serving moralism" to describe ongoing crises that may well warrant international response. Richard Falk warns of the distortion expressed when writers in the countries who are intervening cast themselves in the role of moral saviours of peoples trapped in barbaric circumstances. What such apologists for imperial prerogatives uniformly ignore is the historical record of cruel criminality on the part of these self-appointed, post-colonial guardians of world order. They also ignore the latter's post-intervention record of irresponsible withdrawal or engagement with exploitative forms of reconstruction that ensure strategic control and economic benefits by way of lucrative investment contracts.[35]

Given these legitimate concerns, the Commission focused on "the responsibility to protect" rather than the legitimacy of humanitarian intervention. Beginning with the latter all too readily elides the critical work required, assuming that national self-interest is checked and that the needs of innocent people for protection are paramount.[36]

Furthermore, even if national independence is not breached, peacekeepers themselves may commit violent crimes and sexual assault. According to the 2005 Human Security Report, while the successes of peacekeeping and peacebuilding operations are promising, there are intrinsic dangers that require sustained attention and systematic response. UN peacekeepers were found guilty of rape and the sexual coercion of women and girls in Guinea, Liberia, Sierra Leone, and the Democratic Republic of Congo. As is the case with domestic police forces, the peacekeepers themselves must also be carefully trained and policed![37]

The Responsibility to Protect

Some scholars argue that given these risks, intervention may never be worth the damage that it is likely to cause. Furthermore, the members of the Commission acknowledged that military intervention may create more instability than stability. It may increase "ethnic or civil strife. When internal forces seeking to oppose a state believe that they can generate outside support by mounting campaigns of violence, the internal order of all states is potentially compromised." Here we have a strong assertion of the imperative of the Hippocratic oath: "First, do no harm."[38]

Given these undoubted dangers, the Commission provides a clear description of the moral and political dilemma that we face as global citizens.

> If it [the international community] stays disengaged there is the risk of becoming complicit bystanders in massacre, ethnic cleansing, and even genocide. If the international community intervenes, it may or may not be able to mitigate such abuses. But even when it does, intervention sometimes means taking sides in intra-state conflicts. Once it does so, the international community may only be aiding in the further fragmentation of the state system. Interventions in the Balkans did manage to reduce the civilian death toll, but it has yet to produce a stable state order in the region. As both the Kosovo and Bosnian interventions show, even when the goal of international action is, as it should be, protecting ordinary human beings from gross and systematic abuse, it can be difficult to avoid doing rather more harm than good.[39]

Given these very real and ongoing dangers, let us think back on the situations we are addressing: massacre, ethnic cleansing, genocide. In each of these cases, as in the case of the Holocaust, we do well to heed the admonition of ethicist David Gushee: the "do no harm of the anguished bystander helps the perpetrator far more than the victim of injustice."[40] If we follow the challenge posed by William Schulz, providing ethically rigorous guidance for the use of power, we find ourselves in a moral and political universe limned very clearly by ethicists such as Bonhoeffer and political leaders like Nelson Mandela. Nations act from mixed motives. Our responses to humanitarian crises will never be universal and will rarely be untainted by the self-interest of the intervening parties.

In light of these moral and political realities, the Commission provided this stark guidance: "While aspiring to the ideal of consistency . . . the inevitable double standards of state practice should not be an excuse for paralysis. . . . Even occasionally doing the right thing well is certainly preferable to doing nothing routinely."[41]

How, then, do we act in full awareness of the real risks of failure and the likelihood of abuse? Institutionalized forms of vigilance are required on the macro and micro levels: we need checks both to prevent the exploitation of intervention for national self-interest and on the ground to prevent abuses by security personnel. The former abuses may be checked by vigilance from other nations—requiring that forces leave as soon as possible—and the latter by systemic training in human rights and enforcement of those codes of conduct. It is easier to create such reviews and accept their verdict if, rather than indulge in self-serving moralism, we acknowledge the mixed motives for intervention and do not cast ourselves as noble crusaders against an implacable enemy.

Moral Disengagement

Let us explore one example of the effects that moralistic rhetoric has on preventing serious discussion of the abuses that accompany what is claimed to be humanitarian intervention. Former British Prime Minister Tony Blair was clearly outraged after the first exposure of torture at Abu Ghraib: "Let me make it quite clear that if these things have actually been done, they are completely and totally unacceptable. We went to Iraq to get rid of that sort of thing, not to do it."[42] This outrage was, however, too quickly eroded in the United States by a displacement of responsibility to what were seen as a few ill-trained and misguided soldiers, and the policy decisions by government officials that not only allowed but fostered such abuse and justified torture have yet to be thoroughly and independently investigated. What has led to this erosion of concern?

Social psychologist Albert Bandura has described how easy it is for moral clarity and absolutism to lead to cruelty and violence. Bandura describes seven dimensions of moral disengagement, the process by which genuinely decent human beings commit and justify behaviors that they would otherwise recognize as morally abhorrent. The first factor is being convinced that one is the bearer of a just cause and that there are no other ways of protecting or advancing that cause without some form of coercion. A second dimension is avoiding the negative consequences of one's behavior by distancing oneself from the effects of one's actions. If the effects are not immediately visible, it is relatively easy to deny reports of harm. Third, once negative effects are inescapable, they can be minimized through the use of euphemistic language: for example, the term "collateral damage" for the death and injuries caused to civilians; the terms "professional interrogation techniques" and "softening up prisoners for interrogation" for physical and psychological torture. The negative consequences of one's actions may then be disregarded or denied.

Fourth, when the severity of the consequences can no longer be avoided, one dehumanizes and/or demonizes the victim. We suggest the victims somehow deserve the negative consequences—insinuating, for example, that they are all terrorists or that they all share an irrational hatred of us. A fifth step is advantageous comparison: our violence pales in comparison to theirs. Recall Alberto Gonzales's response when challenged by Senator Lindsay Graham to decisively condemn the use of torture by U.S. personnel: "While we are struggling to try to find out what happened at Abu Ghraib, they're beheading people like Danny Pearl and Nick Berg. We are nothing like our enemy." The sixth and seventh factors are the displacement of responsibility and the diffusion of responsibility: the sense that one was only following orders or acting as can only be expected in "the chaos and fog of war."[43]

These processes of moral disengagement are pervasive and therefore extremely hard to dislodge once in place. Bandura reminds us that humans most often find moral rationales for what others see as immoral acts. We see ourselves as "fighting ruthless oppressors, protecting . . . cherished values, preserving world peace," but we "condemn those [militant actions] of their [our] antagonists as barbarity masquerading under a mask of outrageous moral reasoning." This form of self-justification is so widespread that Bandura claims that "the massive threats to human welfare stem mainly from deliberate acts of principle rather than from unrestrained acts of impulse."[44]

How do we rationalize immoral behavior? It is easier to disregard and distort the negative consequences of our actions when we do not experience them directly. We may also develop an elaborate defense of our actions, denying the fact of negative consequences and dismissing the credibility of those who challenge us.

Bandura argues that the most effective check on unethical behavior is the resolute humanization of those who could be perceived as other. He writes of the "striking evidence that most people refuse to behave cruelly, even under unrelenting authoritarian commands, if the situation is personalized by having them inflict pain by direct personal action rather than remotely and they see the suffering they cause." He states that "the affirmation of common humanity can bring out the best in others." Bandura gives as an example the story of the helicopter pilot, Hugh Thompson, who came upon the My Lai massacre in Vietnam and helped airlift surviving villagers to safety. In this massacre, villagers, women, children, and old men were killed by United States troops. Unlike those who saw only enemies, Thompson "was moved to proactive moral action by the sight of a terrified woman with a baby in her arms and a child clinging to her leg." Bandura cites Thompson's sense of common humanity: "These people were looking at me for help and there is no way I could turn my back on them." He was moved by the sight of a two-year-old boy found holding his dead mother: "I had a son at home about the same age."[45]

Bandura highlights several elements that lead to moral engagement rather than disengagement. It is possible for people to "take personal responsibility for the consequences of their actions; remain sensitive to the suffering of others; and see human commonalities rather than distance themselves from others or divest them of human qualities."[46] With this recognition of the process of moral disengagement, practiced by individuals and by leaders alike, we may be able to meet the goal articulated by William Schulz: Given that it is possible to train people to become torturers, "is it likewise possible to inoculate military, security, or police authorities against becoming human rights violators?" Marc DuBois, an attorney from New Orleans who has been involved in human rights training for police officers, has found that such training is beneficial. He argues that we may be less likely to justify neocolonial domination if we acknowledge the ways in which police and military forces defended colonial power and explore the ways in which the colonial powers used moral reasoning to justify their control.[47]

Just War Tradition

This line of reasoning both places us within the constraints of the just war tradition and amplifies the urgency of those constraints. Let us take as a guiding assumption the stark reality acknowledged by Schulz: the use of violence, even for the best motives, is morally dangerous. In such actions we are, as he so clearly states, "indulging our baser impulses to keep others from indulging theirs." We need, therefore, in addition to the typical constraints of just war traditions, a reminder of the *reason* for those constraints: we are not immune from the use of violence for narrow self-interest, nor immune from the brutal cruelty of unchecked power.[48]

The Commission provided a clear application of traditional just war criteria to the responsibility to protect: right intention, last resort, proportional means, and reasonable prospects.

> Our purpose is not to license aggression with fine words, or to provide strong states with new rationales for doubtful strategic designs, but to strengthen the order of states by providing for clear guidelines to guide

concerted international action in those exceptional circumstances when violence within a state menaces all
peoples.[49]

In their discussion of "right intention," they ask us
to be aware of the intrinsic capacity for abuse, of international actors using military force to "alter borders,"
to "advance the cause of one particular group," or to
"overthrow a particular regime." Likewise, adherence
to the principal of "proportional means" requires that
"the scale, duration and intensity of the planned military intervention should be the minimum necessary to
secure the humanitarian objective in question."[50] While
this principal seems self-evident, it is important to
remember the warning of Schulz and the theory of Bandura: cruelty can be intoxicating. The use of violence,
even for noble ends, can spark excessive violence even
among peacekeepers.

International Consensus

While the challenges of fulfilling the "responsibility to
protect" are daunting, there is increasing openness to
exploring these possibilities. Schulz's directness with
regard to the need for humanitarian intervention may
have been shocking. His forthright acknowledgment
that effective peacekeeping requires the judicious use of
force is certainly unique. The substance of his claim is
widely shared, however, not only by advocates of just
war but also by many Catholic peacemakers and members of historic peace churches, both Mennonites and
Quakers.

In a letter signed June 11, 2007, thirty-eight organizations wrote in support of the resolution before the

United States House that calls for the establishment of a United Nations Emergency Service. Among the nongovernmental organizations were several religious organizations, including the Unitarian Universalist Association of Congregations, the United Church of Christ's Justice and Witness Ministries, the Global Ministries of the Christian Church (Disciples of Christ), and the Presbyterian Church (USA) Washington Office.[51]

Such work is also supported by some members of historical peace churches, long known for their support of nonviolent direct action and opposition to the use of violence in any form. In a publication entitled *Peaceful Prevention of Deadly Conflict*, the Friends Committee on National Legislation reassert their commitment to "a world free of war and the threat of war." In addition to their support of disarmament and advocacy of a wide range of preventive and restorative peacebuilding activities, they also support the formation of "an international civilian police corps."[52] Peacekeeping forces are also supported by the multifaith organization Religions for Peace.[53] And in *Ethics for the New Millennium*, the Dalai Lama provides a description of a goal shared by many who are committed to sustainable peace. He advocates the formation of a globally administered police force with the following mandate:

The main purpose of this force would be to safeguard justice, communal security, and human rights worldwide. Its specific duties would be various, however. Protecting against the appropriation of power by violent means would be one of them . . . it would be called in either by communities which came under threat—from neighbors or from some of its own members, such as a violently extreme political faction—or it could be deployed by the international community itself when violence seemed the likely outcome of conflict, for example, of religious or ideological disputes.[54]

The Dalai Lama predicts that there might be a time in which such multilateral police forces would gradually replace standing armies. He acknowledges that this ultimate goal might not be achieved within our lifetimes but reminds us that we have already initiated this promising work: "Maybe this generation will not live to see it. But we are already accustomed to seeing United Nations troops deployed as peacekeepers. We are also beginning to see the emergence of a consensus that under certain circumstances it may be justifiable to use them in a more interventionist way."[55]

Does the acceptance of the judicious use of force in the case of genocide and crimes against humanity mean that the criticism of violence, and its grave cost to perpetrators and victims, is irrelevant or invalid? Not at all. In the case of the emerging global security system, while the use of some forms of force is accepted as necessary, this reliance on limited violence does not have the valence and power that it does in either holy war, or even just war, where force is seen as the apotheosis of strength and power. In the case of multifaceted, strategic peacekeeping, while force may at times be necessary, it is never sufficient. The value of peacekeeping is not in resolving a conflict, but in providing the space in which enduring security and sustainable peace may be created through the long-term nonviolent work of obtaining comprehensive political assent and participation. Let us turn to a closer examination of these multifaceted tasks—the work of peacemaking and peacebuilding.

2

Peacemaking

At all levels of society, from teachers in elementary schools to heads of state, people are exploring new forms of conflict resolution and mediation. Former enemies have come together in Truth and Reconciliation Commissions in South Africa, Liberia, El Salvador, and fourteen other countries throughout the world, finding ways to openly confront the atrocities of armed conflict and sustained injustice. In societies long divided into warring factions, people are seeking a new national story of mutual accountability and shared commitment to the common good.

The work of ending violence and preventing future armed conflict requires the participation of people at all levels of society, from governmental leaders to members of political parties and religious groups, soldiers, and citizens. And the goal of these activists is far more than the mere cessation of violence or the support of unjust status quo. Political scientists Michael Doyle and Nicholas Sambanis explain that the goal is a sustainable peace characterized by "political assent and the participation of all parties involved."[1] Sustainable peace occurs through the work of what is called Track One diplomacy, officially sanctioned governmental negotiations and policy initiatives, and through the efforts of Track Two diplomacy, the work of civilians at all levels of society to reach new understandings of and find non-violent ways to resolve conflicts.

Track One Diplomacy

Doyle and Sambanis have provided a critical analysis of the success and failures of some of the most notable forms of Track One diplomacy: the peace operations conducted by the United Nations since 1945. They found that the most successful peace accords emerged through a combination of peacemaking, peacekeeping, and peacebuilding activities.

> By expanding the scope of Cold War peacekeeping opera-tions to include units to organize and monitor elections, investigate human rights abuses, train national police forces, and encourage economic redevelopment, recent operations in Mozambique, Cambodia, and El Salvador have transformed bloody civil wars into democratic elections. Discrete, impartial force sometimes made the difference, but at no point did the peacekeepers rely pri-marily on force, as they did in both Bosnia and Somalia, to impose outcomes, thereby making war.[2]

We have already considered the vital role of peace-keeping—defined as stopping direct violence through the "containment and demobilization of military forces." In this chapter we turn to two other ingredients of endur-ing security and sustainable peace: peacemaking and peacebuilding. Peacemaking is the negotiation of peace accords between the different parties to a conflict. Peacebuilding is both preventive and restorative, the creation of long-term structures for redressing injustice and resolving conflicts nonviolently.[3]

Comprehensive Peace Accords

What does it take to reach a comprehensive peace accord? And what are the common elements of sustainable peace agreements? It is often extremely difficult for parties to move from armed conflict to the negotiating conference. In fact, many parties turn to negotiation only after they have reached a "hurting stalemate"—each of the factions aware that military victory is not in sight. Even if none of the parties has any confidence in being able to prevail militarily, they may continue to fight if fighting remains profitable. Doyle and Sambanis claim, for example, that this was the case in Angola: one party to the conflict—General Savimbi's UNITA—profiting from the sale of diamonds to fund military activity, and another party to the conflict—Prime Minister Neto's MPLA—profiting from the sale of oil.[4]

Quite often, political and military leaders will only forgo continued warfare and turn to negotiations when there is sustained pressure both internally and externally. Doyle and Sambanis describe the role played by the "Friends of the Secretary General." These are groups of nations that work to encourage their allies to begin negotiations, to negotiate in good faith, and to accept the terms of an equitable peace accord. At times, such efforts are successful: "In Cambodia, the USSR and China are said to have let their respective clients in Phnom Penh and the Khmer Rouge know that ongoing levels of financial and military support would not be forthcoming if they resisted the terms of a peace treaty that their patrons found acceptable." In El Salvador, the countries of Venezuela, Mexico, Spain, and Colombia, along with the frequent involvement of the United States, played pivotal roles in ending that civil war. In other situations, such as that of Cyprus, international pressure has been ineffective.[5]

Doyle and Sambanis highlight key functions played by such ad hoc diplomatic efforts. They are vital in increasing the influence of the secretary general, demonstrating the support of key allies for putting an end to fighting and reaching a negotiated peace. Furthermore, the terms of such a peace accord are more likely to be accepted by all parties when multiple actors are involved. Multilateral involvement is seen as more legitimate than bilateral efforts, which are often perceived as reflecting particular national interests. Allies can also play a crucial role in mediating the conflict in that they have access to particular parties, can make sure that their interests are represented, and are able to communicate more openly with them. Doyle and Sambanis observe, "It often turns out that one particular 'Friend' can associate with one faction just as another associates with a second. In the Cambodian peace process, China backstopped the Khmer Rouge just as France did Prince Sihanouk and Russia (with Vietnam) did the State of Cambodia. The Friends open more flexible channels of communication than a single UN mediator can provide."[6]

What J. K. Gibson-Graham find true in building community economies is equally true in reaching sustainable peace accords. Successful negotiators "begin where they are and build on what they have."[7] In any conflict, the United Nations and the Friends of the Secretary General try to utilize the resources for stability and equity that are currently available. Doyle and Sambanis refer to these as "three critical dimensions of the peace-building triangle." Negotiators help parties in conflict identify (1) sources of cultural unity and understanding, whether informal or formal, as well as (2) "an industrial base or other economic activity that can sustain the country without humanitarian assistance or other foreign economic aid." Negotiators also work with the international community to ensure (3) adequate investment by the international community in the peace process itself, as well as financial support to address basic economic needs.[8]

Multiple actors are required and creative thinking is necessary to reach a comprehensive peace accord. Such an accord involves far more than a truce between warring factions, incorporating instead an acceptable and feasible set of "terms on which the once warring parties are prepared to live in peace with each other." Often, these terms require an intermediary role for the United Nations and other international agencies, from ongoing humanitarian relief, to security sector reform, to even a "transitional international authority" to govern the country as it moves from war to peace.[9]

Doyle and Sambanis remind us of the magnitude of the social changes required for sustainable peace. The damage caused by civil war is massive and long lasting: "Civil wars . . . break up sovereignty and then sometimes create ferocious hierarchies in factions. Warriors, sometimes criminals, replace civil elites. Economies become geared to military production or looting. Hatred shapes interethnic or factional identity."[10]

These threats to national stability are not quickly or readily restrained. Sometimes it may be necessary to reorganize the very nature of the state, dividing the country or establishing new political parties. Former enemies must learn to live together in a common polity, economy, and culture. Such changes can easily take over a decade. The magnitude of what is required can be seen in the case of the United States after the Civil War. Doyle and Sambanis remind us of the stark facts of that protracted struggle. "The U.S. Civil War took ten years—until the compromise of 1876—to establish a sustainable peace that allowed the end of the occupation, but then only on terms that were not sustainable in terms of American principles."[11]

Author and professor Nicholas Lemman describes the ugly story of "Redemption," the last battle of the U.S. Civil War. "'Redemption' was the word that white Southerners chose to describe their violent attacks on black citizens who tried to exercise their newly won rights to vote and hold property," explains Lemman. "The leaders of the successful campaign of political violence, defiance of the national government, and local repeal of parts of the Constitution called themselves 'Redeemers.'" In a two-year period from 1873 to 1875, former members of the Confederacy took "their homeland back from what they saw as a formidable misalliance of the federal government and the Negro. The drama of it was so powerful that killing defenseless people registered in their minds as acts of bravery." The amount of violence was staggering. In the span of a single year, 2,141 African Americans were killed in Louisiana, and 2,115 were wounded. The white perpetrators of these crimes not only went unpunished but were lauded as heroes by white Southerners resisting equal political and economic rights for African American citizens. While many in the South supported the work of "Redemption," others recognized the severity of the crisis. President Grant, for example, decried the horror of one assault by whites on African American citizens: "A butchery of citizens was committed at Colfax, which in blood-thirstiness and barbarity is hardly surpassed by any acts of savage warfare." Despite such justified outrage, the federal government failed to provide the

ongoing economic, military, and cultural support necessary to ensure even the basic safety—much less the full
human rights—of African American citizens. This "last
battle of the Civil War" had momentous effects.[12] Doyle
and Sambanis conclude that the United States did not
reach a sustainable peace accord until "a hundred years
after the end of the war, with the victory of the civil
rights movement."[13]

People across the political spectrum are beginning
to learn from history and recognize that the task of
post-conflict reconstruction is as vital as ending armed
violence. With the concerted involvement of the international community, it may be possible to reach a sustainable peace in a matter of years rather than decades.
According to Doyle and Sambanis, for example, the civil
war in El Salvador (1979–1990) emerged out of political conflicts that had existed for over a hundred years.
By 1980 there was armed conflict between the FMLN
(four political military organizations plus the Commu-
nist Party of El Salvador), the government of El Salvador, and right-wing death squads. During the period
of military conflict "over 75,000 lives were lost and
more than 1 million people—almost one-quarter of the
population—had been displaced."[14]

In 1983, an ad hoc group of Latin American countries called the Contadora Group—comprised of Colombia, Mexico, Panama, and Venezuela—first persuaded
other regional governments not to support either the
insurrection or the government. The UN began to patrol
the borders to enforce this agreement. In 1989 dialogue
began between the government and the FMLN. When
fighting resumed, both the government and FMLN,
with the support of five Central American presidents,
"separately requested the diplomatic intervention by

the Secretary-General." Over a period of three years, a series of peace accords led to significant changes in El Salvadoran society. The FMLN became a fully recognized political party, and there were significant reforms of the judiciary, the military, and the electoral system. In addition, the Truth Commission was established to bring to justice those involved in death squads. Despite these political changes, the seeds of future conflict remain unredressed. Doyle and Sambanis note the continuing "deep social inequities, inadequate land reform, and a wave of criminal activity by illegal vigilante groups."[15]

Although peace accords cannot in themselves redress all of the social injustices that led to the conflict in the first place, they can serve as a platform, as bridges to the political and cultural resolution of ongoing conflicts. John Paul Lederach is known worldwide for his work as a mediator in Nicaragua, Northern Ireland, Tajikistan, and the Philippines. Lederach claims that the best-negotiated settlements function as platforms: they serve as a framework for continued reconciliation, restoration, and the building of a social order in which conflicts are settled without violence.[16]

Lederach reminds us of the limited yet essential role of peace accords. Such accords have the immediate goal of stopping violence, and they lay the foundation for the "deeper transformation" required to establish a lasting peace. He claims that confidence slowly increases, step by step, as opposing parties agree first on measures such as "ceasefires, the exchange of prisoners, territorial protection or retreat, or the reduction of troops." It is only after these partial steps that the ongoing work of peacebuilding can begin, finding ways of building just political, social, and economic structures and establishing the means and collective will to resolve ongoing conflicts within the framework of the rule of law.[17]

Track Two Diplomacy

Historian and journalist Jos Havermans states that reaching such a comprehensive basis for ongoing negotiation requires not just the involvement of political leaders, but the active support of citizens from all sectors of society. While peace accords cannot be created without the work of political leaders, they cannot be implemented and sustained without popular support. The work of nongovernmental organizations and individuals is required both to end the fighting and to implement a sustainable peace accord. As Havermans reminds us, regardless of the agreements made by the government and the leaders of warring factions, "other actors, local leaders or rebel groups may decide to continue fighting." Nongovernmental organizations and individuals can refuse to support such ongoing violence. They can also "take risks and try new ideas, difficult for leaders."[18] Paul van Tongeren, executive director of the European Centre for Conflict Prevention, describes the dramatic increase in the numbers of people working at all levels of society to resolve conflict. He extols the flourishing of multitrack diplomacy: "Churches, women's organizations, the media and business have all demonstrated their potential for building peace."[19]

Havermans also highlights the importance of deliberately and systematically integrating the work of formal and informal diplomacy. The Canadian government, for example, established a Canadian Peacebuilding Program in 1999 within the Department of Foreign Affairs. The Canadian Peacebuilding Program coordinates "a comprehensive peace building strategy, consisting of support to nongovernmental peace organizations and plans to prepare government agencies, including the armed forces, for tasks in the field of peace building, conflict management, [and] mediation."[20]

Without popular support, peace accords will fail. It is often, however, extremely difficult to find terms of agreement that are seen as just, as feasible, and as inspiring to all parties to a conflict. The resistance to a specific form of peaceful coexistence is often as great as the longing for an end to violence. Based on his many years of experience in negotiating peace accords, John Paul Lederach describes the challenge of working with such resistance and discerning the wisdom that it conveys. Resistance to proposed political change can be seen as a gift, not as an obstacle to lasting change. It may be a realistic reminder of what is required for change to be seen as equitable, authentic, and grounded in the history, stories, and aspirations of particular cultures and peoples. He lists five statements that reflect a "well-grounded realism" about what is required to heal deep social and economic disparities:

1. Change . . . does not come easy.
2. Change does not come quickly. Be suspicious of any body with a quick fix solution. It is usually a trap.
3. Judge the change by decades if not generations.
4. Words are cheap. . . . Don't expect a piece of paper signed by politicians to change your life.
5. To survive violence, create walls and retrench. . . . Don't give up your walls too easily. You will likely live to regret it.[21]

Although often dispiriting to those working for peace, these statements may reflect a well-grounded understanding of the complexity and long time frame required for durable peacebuilding. Lederach claims that lasting change emerges out of a specific historical situation, not in spite of that situation. As Lederach says, peacemakers are involved in the art of acknowledging, understanding, and "responding to historical patterns [without being] bound by them." Peacemakers deliberately bring together people who have different interpretations of their common past, groups with different experiences, and—rather than trying to get one group to accept the narrative and interpretation of the other—try to find ways to create new relationships and develop new understandings of the interdependence that shapes them and the future they may share. As Lederach observes, "Constructive change and peace are not built by attempting to win converts to one side or another, or by forcing one or the other's hand." He claims that the goal of peacemakers is not the implementation of a utopian ideal, but the forging of "relational spaces that have not existed or that must be strengthened."[22]

According to Lederach, if we take these concerns seriously and attempt to work with resistance to change, we find ourselves participating in a paradigm shift—a new understanding of what peacemaking and peace accords can and cannot accomplish:

> The war is over, formal negotiations concluded, and changes have come usually in terms of increased space for political participation. However, the expectations for social, economic, religious and cultural change are rarely achieved, creating a gap between the expectations for peace and what it delivered.[23]

Peacemaking creates the space in which participatory peace may be forged. Addressing the legitimate expectations for fundamental social and economic change requires far more than negotiated settlements. It requires the long-term work of peacebuilding.

3

Peacebuilding

In *The Little Book of Strategic Peacebuilding*, Lisa Schirch reflects on her experience of working for fifteen years in peacebuilding activities in the United States, Latin America, Africa, Asia, the South Pacific, and Europe. Schirch has worked in a refugee camp, has organized human rights campaigns, has been a civilian peacekeeper, has worked on rural economic development, and has extensive experience as a mediator. She is clear about the nature and scope of the political activities that we wish to sustain and evoke as alternatives to military intervention. She calls these activities, taken as a whole, *strategic* peacebuilding and describes four components of this work: (1) waging conflict nonviolently, (2) reducing direct violence, (3) transforming relationships, and (4) building capacity to meet basic needs and protect human rights.[1]

By speaking of "strategic peacebuilding," Schirch and others highlight the deliberate, sustained activities that are required to build enduring security and sustainable peace: the complex work of "long term planning, anticipating potential problems, engaging in ongoing analysis of the conflict and local context, and coordinating different actors and activities."[2] In chapter 1, we addressed the challenge of reducing direct violence through peacekeeping, and in chapter 2, the task of peacemaking: reaching comprehensive peace accords. We now move to the other three dimensions of strategic peacebuilding identified by Schirch: waging conflict nonviolently, building capacity to meet basic needs, and transforming relationships. This is work that is preventive as well as restorative, constructive as well as critical. It is the long-term work of building peace.

Transforming Relationships through Restorative Justice

Justice is not met solely with the cessation of war, nor by a more equitable division of political power and economic wealth. Lasting justice is attained through restitution, reconciliation, and reintegration. Restorative justice acknowledges the trauma caused to individuals and to the collective identity of a people and a nation. It addresses the very real danger of ongoing cycles of victimization and revenge.[3]

Ikechi Mgbeoji, professor of law, in *Collective Insecurity: The Liberian Crisis, Unilateralism, and Global Order*, writes of the imperative and the magnitude of the task of reconciliation. He recounts the atrocities committed by child soldiers and by adults in the civil war in Liberia, and the importance for accountability and restoration of justice: "According to the testimony of one of the child-soldiers, 'I was given pills that made me crazy. I beat people and hurt them until they bled.'"[4]

Recall the quote in William Schulz's foreword from one person who participated in the atrocities in Rwanda: "A car drove by with a loudspeaker saying that all Hutus had to defend themselves, that there was a single enemy:

the Tutsi. I heard that. I jumped out of bed, grabbed a club, I went out, and I began killing."[5]

In the aftermath of such violence, a society is faced with the daunting challenge of finding cultural and judicial resources to enable people to acknowledge the magnitude of what has been lost. It is faced with the imperative of crafting rituals of collective rage and mourning without succumbing to new cycles of hatred, victimization, and revenge. A lasting peace requires that those who were at war learn to live as fellow citizens: militias disarmed, leaders held accountable, and former combatants reintegrated into the larger society.

According to the Commission on International Security, the reintegration of former soldiers into society is a multidimensional task: economic—jobs and alternate sources of income must be provided; cultural/religious—rituals of forgiveness and healing are implemented or created that allow former antagonists to live and work together for a common good; political—competing forces are integrated into a newly unified political system; and judicial—war criminals are identified and prosecuted.[6]

Kees Kingma, project leader for demobilization and peacebuilding at the Bonn International Center for Conversion in Germany, also addresses the complex tasks of the disarmament, demobilization, and reintegration of combatants. Kingma claims that in addition to combatants' receiving economic help and returning weapons, far more is needed to show that the social order is being restored. He gives an example from Mozambique, a case in which many former soldiers spent much of their demobilization money on gifts to village elders. They also participated in cleansing rituals conducted by the elders and the community. Kingma acknowledges that economic aid to former combatants is important, yet he claims that it is equally important that reintegration be done in a way to benefit the entire community. For example, such aid can be used to provide support for the families of combatants, for the victims of rape, and for the child soldiers who have experienced trauma, taken from their families and forced not only to witness but to commit atrocities.[7]

Lisa Schirch helps us understand the magnitude of the work of reconciliation. In healing a society after violent conflict, both restorative and transitional justice are of the utmost importance. Restorative justice addresses the individual and social obligations borne by the perpetrators of social injustice and violence. Transitional justice involves the creation of new judicial systems to replace systems that were corrupt or ineffective.[8]

Truth commissions and war crime tribunals are designed to address the need for restorative justice. Lederach gives a concise description of the overarching purpose of such commissions: They "create a public and system-wide accountability for crimes and atrocities committed within the period of recent violence. . . . [They] bring into the public sphere a collective acknowledgment of what happened, who suffered, who was responsible, and how they are accountable."[9]

Although there is widespread international support for such commissions and tribunals, we have much to learn about the process of reaching reconciliation. As Lederach states, this is not just a matter "of establishing individual guilt or innocence" but of collective efforts to "renegotiate history and identity."[10] The perpetrators of atrocities do not act alone. Ratko Mladic, for example, the Bosnian general "who waged the siege of Sarajevo and is accused of engineering the massacre [of eight thousand Muslim men and boys] at Srebrenica" is sought by the International Criminal Court, yet is still revered as a hero by many Serbs.[11]

Michelle Parlevliet—program manager of a human rights and conflict management training program in South Africa—describes a shift in the practice of truth commissions seeking to achieve restorative justice. Truth commissions, she explains, began as a way of dealing "with a legacy of abuses because the political circumstances often precluded bringing perpetrators to justice. 'Bringing truth to light' then at least ensured that knowledge of past crimes would be preserved." Crimes that were denied and ignored, "such as disappearances, torture, killings by anonymous death squads," are now acknowledged. This lays the ground for further work—work crucial to a new social order. Parlevliet recounts the value of the truth commissions in South Africa. Because of their work, the government and the population as a whole have had to admit that there was systematic torture by police and military personnel, and such torture was neither investigated nor punished. Even if torture was not directly ordered by the state, it was condoned by the state and by society. Such recognition brings to light what was done in the past and also makes it possible for a society to discern what must be done in order to prevent such brutality in the future. What reforms of the security sector and judicial system are essential? What changes are required to transform a culture of impunity and hatred that fostered such violence?[12]

Schirch and Lederach find that the depth of pain experienced in the past, the poignancy of hopes for a better present and future, and the fear and longing that accompany such social transformation are often best expressed in art and ritual. These are forms of expression that enable us to see the magnitude of what is at stake—forms of expression that remind us of the resilience and creativity that may grace our communities in even the direst circumstances and most daunting situations.[13]

Waging Conflict Nonviolently
Conflict Transformation

The goal of strategic peacebuilding is to prevent violence and war, not to prevent conflict. Conflict is endemic to human existence. Sometimes grievances are justified, as in cases of structural violence, and sometimes not. In either situation, we need ongoing cultural and institutional mechanisms for engaging conflict equitably and creatively. Lederach prefers using the term "conflict transformation" for this work rather than either conflict resolution or conflict management. He began using the former term in the 1980s, after his work in Central America. His coworkers there helped him understand not only that conflict is a normal part of individual and social relationships, but that "conflict is often a motor of change." By speaking of conflict transformation, he highlights the salient fact that conflicts are often a manifestation of the need for real change, whether it be between individuals or between social groups.[14]

Lederach describes four goals of conflict transformation: First, individuals turn to conflict transformation because they want to "minimize the destructive effects of social conflict" and "maximize opportunities" for well-being. Second, individuals have "relational goals," the hope of reaching a greater understanding of the fears and hopes of the parties to the conflict, an honest appraisal of the ways in which groups are interdependent, and a recognition of the ways in which their decisions effect each other, for good or for ill. Third, for the society as a whole, there are the structural goals of redressing the economic and political root causes of conflict, rectifying inequitable patterns of political participation, and reforming economic structures when they fail to meet basic human needs. And finally, Lederach claims that there is a complex series of cultural dimensions of conflict. He states that people can learn to see the cultural patterns that lead to violence, identifying destructive perceptions of enmity, compromise, even conflict itself. At times, compromise may be seen as failure—and only decisive defeat of enemies seen as success. People may also discover alternative cultural resources that acknowledge the ways in which peoples are connected and that embody respect for the traditions and histories of others. At this point, it becomes possible to develop terms of living together in which peace is not capitulation but is a viable strategy for long-term security and vital coexistence.[15]

Since conflicts are a natural part of human relationships, regular means of redressing conflicts are needed, both nationally and internationally. The entire judicial system of a country may have been corrupt before the conflict, in which case such corruption may have been a precipitating factor in the outbreak of violence, or it may have become corrupt, used for partisan purposes in the course of civil war. In order to address these situations, many nongovernmental organizations have developed standard penal codes that can be applied immediately, "protecting minority rights, and detaining those who commit crime," thereby providing needed stability as the rule of law is restored or created.[16]

While creating or restoring the rule of law within a country is essential, the international community faces another challenge, that of establishing and implementing the rule of law between nations. It is quite likely that the proposal for an international rule of law was utopian when first raised as a possibility for European nations by Kant and Erasmus. When Kant called for the rule of law as the foundation of an enduring peace, and when Erasmus asked for international councils to arbitrate the conflicts between Christian princes, the rule of law was barely established within nations, much less between nations.[17] Now, however, the rule of law is taken for granted as the foundation of civil order within nations, and there are movements by many countries to establish the rule of law between nations. On July 1, 2002, the Rome Statute established the International Criminal Court, an autonomous institution, not part of the United Nations, located in The Hague, Netherlands. The International Criminal Court has been ratified "by most democratic nations and all European Union countries, along with Canada, New Zealand, and a number of African, Eastern European and central Asian countries." The ICC has eighteen judges and is overseen by an assembly made up of one representative of every country that has signed the Rome Statute.

The ICC is responsible for prosecuting individuals accused of genocide, crimes against humanity, and war crimes in cases where national courts cannot or will not prosecute such crimes.[18] Crimes against humanity include "any of the following acts when committed as part of a widespread or systematic attack directed against any civilian population": the trafficking of women and children, the withholding of food and medicine, ethnic cleansing, rape, enforced prostitution, enforced sterilization, or the disappearance of persons. War crimes include such actions as directing attacks against civilians, peacekeepers, and humanitarian workers; impeding relief supplies; rape; and enforced sterilization.[19]

The ICC has begun investigations in four countries: Uganda, the Democratic Republic of the Congo, the Central African Republic, and Darfur. The government of Uganda asked the court to help investigate war crimes in which over twenty thousand children have been abducted by rebels to serve as child soldiers and sex slaves. The government of the Democratic Republic of Congo has asked for help in investigating and prosecuting the militias who are raping and massacring thousands of civilians. In Darfur, while the government continues to deny that genocide is occurring, the UN Security Council has referred these crimes to the ICC.[20]

While not yet accepted by the United States government, the ICC has widespread international support and widespread popular support, even within the United States. The ICC may well prove to be a viable alternative to military intervention, a multilateral way of bringing to justice those guilty of humanity's gravest crimes.[21]

Nonviolent Direct Action to Challenge Structural Violence

What are our options, however, as citizens committed to social justice, when we find ourselves in situations in which the rule of law is not yet fully employed to redress structural violence? What are nonviolent means of resolving conflicts when normal political processes and regular judicial remedies are inadequate or unfairly applied?

In addition to the threat of direct violence, structural violence may seriously disrupt the peace of a society. Structural violence refers to the damage caused to individuals and groups from institutionalized forms of exclusion and marginalization. In *Witness to War*, Charlie Clements, director of the Unitarian Universalist Service Committee, recounts a conversation in which he was challenged by a peasant in El Salvador:

> You gringos are always worried about violence done
> with machine guns and machetes. But there is another
> kind of violence you should be aware of too. I used to
> work on the hacienda. . . . My job was to take care of the
> *dueño*'s dogs. I gave them meat and bowls of milk, food
> that I couldn't give my own family. When the dogs were
> sick, I took them to the veterinarian in Suchitoto or
> San Salvador. When my children were sick, the *dueño*
> gave me his sympathy but no medicine as they died. To
> watch your children die of sickness and hunger while
> you can do nothing is a violence to the spirit. We have
> suffered silently for too many years. Why aren't you
> gringos concerned about that kind of violence?[22]

We can better understand the complexity and per-
vasiveness of structural violence by examining the five
forms of oppression delineated by political scientist Iris
Marion Young in *Justice and the Politics of Difference*.
Young claims that in order for a society to be just, it is
crucial to understand the varied forms in which racism, sexism, homophobia, and the oppression of ethnic
and religious groups are expressed. One common form
of oppression is exploitation: "a steady process of the
transfer of the results of the labor of one social group to
benefit another."[23] Throughout the world, many factory
workers, agricultural laborers, and people in the service
industry are chronically overworked and underpaid.

A second form of oppression is marginalization:
"Marginals are people the system of labor cannot or will
not use." In addition to not being employed, people who
are marginalized are often treated disrespectfully by the
social agencies designed to serve them. They are also
often viewed as extraneous to the social and political
system, their ideas having little weight or value. In the
U.S., for example, the elderly, people with disabilities,

single mothers, people on welfare, the inner-city poor, and Native American people on reservations are all subject to marginalization.[24]

A third form of oppression is powerlessness: "The powerless have little or no work autonomy, exercise little creativity or judgment in their work, have no technical expertise or authority . . . [and] do not command respect."[25] Many working-class and middle-class people experience this form of injustice. Although able to earn a living wage, many do not receive social status or respect for their work as teachers, nurses, farmers, electricians, plumbers, and mechanics.

A fourth form of oppression is cultural imperialism: "the universalisation of a dominant group's experience and culture, and its establishment as the norm. . . . To experience cultural imperialism means to experience how the dominant meanings of a society render the particular perspective of one's own group invisible at the same time as they stereotype one's group and mark it out as the Other."[26] This form of oppression—the stereotypes of women and people of color in textbooks, advertising, and television—is only seemingly innocuous. It reflects and perpetuates deeply held patterns of aversion and invisibility, marring the ability of all citizens in a country to be seen in their individuality and complexity, to be valued as citizens, as workers, as shapers of our common story.

A fifth form of oppression is more obvious and well recognized: direct violence. As Young explains, "Members of some groups live with the knowledge that they must fear random, unprovoked attacks on their persons or property, which have no motive but to damage, humiliate, or destroy the person."[27] Our contemporary world is rife with such violence: racially motivated attacks against African Americans and Muslims, the fear that women have of rape, the fear that people who are gay and lesbian have of physical assault.

What does it take to challenge these forms of structural violence? How do we address structural disparities between ideals of reason, justice, and equality? How might we counter the institutionalized practices of denying fundamental rights to certain groups of people?

We still have much to learn from the nonviolent campaigns led by Mahatma Gandhi and Martin Luther King Jr. According to Gandhi, the goal of nonviolent action—what he called satyagraha, or truth/soul force—is threefold:

(a) To enlist the support of others: "An awakened and intelligent public opinion is the most potent weapon of a Satyagrahi [practitioner of nonviolence]."

(b) To ensure the perpetrator loses moral authority and support.

(c) To help the perpetrators see the costs of their violence and choose to stop. Gandhi writes, "It is never the intention of a Satyagrahi to embarrass the wrong-doer. The appeal is never to his fear; it is, must be, always to his heart. The Satyagrahi's object is to convert, not to coerce."[28]

In Gandhi's campaigns for social justice in South Africa and in India, we find a clear focus: he is not opposed to particular individuals or peoples as such, but rather the injustice of their violent and exploitative rule. His goal is not their defeat but their transformation.[29]

In order to accomplish this goal of transformation, Gandhi advocated a close correspondence between means and ends. He urged that a Satyagrahi adhere to the following means:

a) *Constant vigilance.* In challenging and resisting evil, do not become that which you are resisting. Gandhi reminded his followers, and himself, that "the only devils in the world are those running around in our own hearts. That is where the battle should be fought." He stated that "a Satyagrahi always tries by close and prayerful self-introspections . . . to find out . . . whether he is himself capable of those very evils against which he is out to lead a crusade." He also asked proponents of Indian independence to always remember the humanity of the opponent: "A Satyagrahi must never forget the distinction between evil and the evil-doer. He must not harbour ill-will or bitterness against the latter. He may not even employ needlessly offensive language against the evil person, however unrelieved his evil might be. For it should be an article of faith with every Satya-grahi that there is none so fallen in this world but can be converted by love. A Satyagrahi will always try to overcome evil by good, anger by love, untruth by truth, himsa by ahimsa."[30]

b) *Avoid violence in thought, word, and deed.* Gandhi reminded us of the power of violent words and the need to find language that appealed to the best of one's opponents—to their full humanity, not to their fear. He contested, therefore, the angry language used by one of his associates in criticizing a statue of the British general Neill: "A Satyagrahi's appeal must contain moderate language. The appeal before us, though unexceptionable, admits of improvement. 'Not only Neill but all of his nefarious breed must go' is a sentence that mars the appeal. . . . Here there is no room for the language of anger and hate."[31]

c) *Active noncooperation with violence.* Such noncooperation entailed remarkable strategic creativity and innovation, finding forms of direct action (such as the Salt March, spinning, and the boycott of English cloth) that defied oppressive economic structures and political regulations.

d) *Courage.* Gandhi spoke often of being willing to die but not to kill and evoked fearlessness and calm under fire.[32]

e) *Discipline.* Gandhi consistently encouraged his followers to transform anger into persistent action. He wrote, "For when tyranny is rampant much rage is generated among the victims. It remains latent because of their weakness and bursts in all its fury on the slightest pretext. Civil disobedience is a sovereign method of transmitting this undisciplined life-destroying latent energy into disciplined life-saving energy whose use ensures absolute success."[33]

Gandhi rejected violence as a means of social change because of his understanding of the difference between human and divine authority and because of his commitment to the law of love. He held firmly to the idea of what was truth without completely knowing the truth: "Satyagraha is literally holding on to Truth and it means, therefore, Truth-force. . . . It excludes the use of violence because man is not capable of knowing the absolute truth and, therefore, not competent to punish."[34] Gandhi was as certain of the truth of the law of love as he was aware of the need to find ways to express that love creatively in particular situations. He wrote, "Indeed the sum total of the experience of mankind is that men somehow or another live on. From which I infer that it is the law of love that rules mankind. Had violence, i.e. hate, ruled us, we should have become extinct long ago. . . . It gives me ineffable joy to make experiments proving that love is the very supreme and only law of life."[35]

Martin Luther King Jr., James Lawson, Bayard Rustin, and other leaders of the civil rights movement were strongly influenced by Gandhi's understanding of the depth and range of nonviolence. Like Gandhi before him, King claimed that

> nonviolence . . . does not seek to defeat or humiliate the opponent, but to win his friendship and understanding. The nonviolent resister must often express his protest through noncooperation or boycotts, but he realizes that these are not ends themselves; they are merely means to awaken a sense of moral shame in the opponent. The end is redemption and reconciliation. The aftermath of nonviolence is the creation of the beloved community, while the aftermath of violence is tragic bitterness.[36]

Gandhi's "experiments with truth" have continued, as have King's attempts to create the "beloved community." Lisa Schirch delineates the core elements in nonviolent direct action, elements seen throughout history, in the work of Gandhi, the civil rights movement, the women's movement, and other movements for human dignity and equality. Schirch claims that nonviolent direct action "escalates conflict without using violence." The goal of direct action is to increase public understanding of the suffering of others and the ways in which that suffering is due to structural injustice, rather than individual failures or natural limitations. Nonviolent direct action also has the goal of "balancing power by convincing or coercing others to accept the needs and desires of all involved."[37]

In her analysis of nonviolent direct action, Schirch makes a point not recognized by many peace activists: nonviolent direct action is a form of coercion and cannot, by itself, establish peace. While it is "essential as structures resist change and people in power . . . ignore pleas for dialogue or negotiation," nonviolent action "escalates conflict and can temporarily increase antagonism and tension between people and groups." Direct action exposes the divisions and inequality in a social order. Further cooperative actions are required to heal those divisions and rectify those inequalities.[38]

Schirch claims that nonviolent direct action can expose violence that is hidden or denied, can intervene in structural violence, and can expose the power of marginalized and exploited groups. She delineates the tactics that expose violence to both its perpetrators and the world community. She writes of the importance of monitoring unjust behavior—always, in a Gandhian spirit, being careful to "shame behaviors rather than people." Like King, she writes of the continued importance of not isolating people but "inviting them into another way of being in community." Protests and other public actions (publications, speeches, marches, symbolic mock funerals) are also effective in exposing the structural violence that many people in a society refuse to acknowledge.[39]

Schirch also claims that nonviolent direct action can effectively intervene in structural violence. Such actions "interrupt an unjust status quo" through "fasts, physically occupying public space, public drama, the strategic overloading of public facilities, setting up alternative economic systems, engaging in acts of civil disobedience and seeking imprisonment for that disobedience, even creating parallel governments."[40] Nonviolent direct action can also intervene through noncooperation with unjust social structures by boycotting social events and by disrupting an unjust economic structure through slowdowns, strikes, and boycotts. Finally, direct action may expose the power of groups seen as powerless. Economic and social boycotts demonstrate the ways in which other groups in the nation depend on their participation, and sanctions by the world community demonstrate that their dignity and welfare are valued by others.[41]

Conflict Prevention: Early Warning

In addition to waging conflict nonviolently, strategic peacebuilding includes preventing violent conflict from erupting. Prevention has two dimensions, one a recognition that grievances are about to erupt and acting to curtail imminent violence, the other more systematic, redressing the root causes of conflict long before they lead to violence. Camille Pampell Conaway and Anjalina Sen describe the importance of paying attention to long-term indicators of crisis such as military rule, political oppression, and economic disparity; medium-term indicators such as the formation of militias, heightened popular discontent, and a rise in unemployment; and immediate indicators such as election fraud, political arrests, crackdown on peaceful demonstrations, detentions, disappearances, forced recruitment into militias, and forced prostitution. While the early warning signs of conflict may be clear, the international community has yet to develop the institutional means of rapid and effective response.[42] To work for peace requires developing such capacity as much as protesting the undue reliance on military force.

Conflict Prevention: Root Causes

A crucial component of strategic peacebuilding is attention to the root causes of civil war, genocide, and crimes against humanity. Conflict can be prevented when societies acknowledge that there is an imbalance in political power and provide full access to the political process and support for the freedom of the press. Conflict can also be prevented by instituting much-needed economic reforms that benefit the entire populace and utilize the leadership of the local community. Human rights professor Arjun Sengupta claims that development is not just a matter of increased income but of increased participation, a social change in which the beneficiaries of development programs have a full role in the creation and implementation of systems that allow more equitable access to water, food, energy, jobs, education, and health care.

Finally, another fundamental cause of conflict is inadequate legal institutions. The international community and groups within a society may help prevent conflict by "supporting efforts to strengthen the rule of law; protecting the integrity and independence of the judiciary; promoting honesty and accountability in law enforcement; enhancing protections for vulnerable groups, especially minorities; and providing support to local institutions and organizations working to advance human rights."[43] Some of the most vulnerable groups are, of course, refugees, and their safe return poses significant political, legal, and economic challenges: provisions must be made for the restoration of tenancy rights, and access must be provided to housing, jobs, and education.[44]

Lisa Schirch states that the work of political, economic, and legal reform also has an educational dimension. How should a society teach about a conflict once it has ended and after peace agreements are signed? As a society engages in far-reaching political reforms, what stories are being told of who we were, who we are, and who we may become?[45]

Failure and Resilience

Lederach describes the challenge of "reweaving a social fabric torn apart by decades and generations of hatred." He addresses the difficulties that communities have in creating sustainable peace and claims that we often "know more about how to end something damaging but less about how to build something desired." Lederach states that a basic tenet of building peace is, therefore, a forthright acknowledgment of the intrinsic limits and challenges of the process of peacebuilding itself. Building a lasting peace requires learning from obstacles and delays and being resilient in the face of defeat and unintended consequences.[46] Not only are the tasks of strategic peacebuilding primarily constructive rather than reactive, but they carry with them the possibility of failure as much as of success. In the work of many peace activists we find a thought-provoking twist on political analysis and activity: the recognition that peacekeepers are also a mix of good and evil, that nonviolence and peacemaking can fail, be coercive, and be used for unjust ends.

Schirch addresses a common cause of political failure: internal conflicts among those working for peace. She claims that conflict occurs as frequently between people who share common goals as between those who have different goals. She writes of the conflicts between peace builders "as they seek funding for projects, as they negotiate with each other about opportunities, and as they seek recognition for their work." She reminds us that the development of "relational skills" are as important for peacebuilders as for anyone else: "Without them, peacebuilding crumbles to interpersonal squabbles among peacebuilders, angry crowds shouting messages of hate, and political decisions made purely on the basis of power rather than on human needs."[47]

Given the intrinsic limitations and dangers of all forms of strategic peacebuilding, it is clear that coordination, efficiency, and assessment of the actual impact of attempts to bring peace and justice are sorely needed. While the use of armed forces can undoubtedly be counterproductive, strategic peacebuilding may also have unintended negative consequences. Lederach gives an example of unintended consequences: the way in which relief efforts can actually exacerbate conflict.

> To deliver food effectively, for example, feeding centers might be established, which have the latent functions of centralizing aid and increasing internal migration. . . . The centralization of resources and migration of vulnerable populations further attracts those who, also living off the scarce resources, seek to benefit from the people's struggle. Aid programs can thus contribute to the mobilization and strengthening of militias. In settings where outside aid is in fact the only available resource, this effect is greatly intensified. In the case of Somalia in the first half of the 1990s, . . . relief aid was sought after, fought over, and ultimately sustained militias, creating a situation in which the delivery of the aid had to be protected.[48]

As builders of peace, we need to take seriously the possibilities that just as the use of force to defeat evil may increase evil, so too may our nonviolent efforts to establish peace exacerbate or fail to remediate serious conflicts.[49]

While some of our failures may be of our own making, there are also external reasons for failure. Here we have another lesson from the work of peacebuilding: the power of violence and the resilience of hatred and enmity. Doyle and Sambanis describe the dangers posed by "spoilers"–those who are benefiting from armed conflict and wish to disrupt the peace process.[50] As we know too well, peace agreements can easily be derailed by individual acts of violence.

Why is it easier to disrupt a peace accord than it is to sustain amity? The reasons are simple yet daunting. According to Lederach, "Authenticity involves a long waiting period until people believe the change is real, but judgment of inauthenticity is continuous and immediate."[51]

In our work for peace, we may be outmaneuvered and overpowered, our efforts to transform a situation derailed by the depth of fear and hatred and by the terrible beauty of compelling community narratives sustained by exclusion, revenge, and violence. While the challenges of building peace are complex, we are not alone in our efforts to create enduring security and sustainable peace. In spite of the difficulties, in spite of the failures, there are avenues of progress. Organizations such as Global Action to Prevent War, the Friends Committee on National Legislation, and the Catholic Peacebuilding Network continue to refine their strategies for resolving conflict without war.[52] The member states of the United Nations have also taken significant steps to build peace, passing resolutions in 2001 and 2003 expressing a commitment to "enhance the effectiveness of the United Nations in addressing conflict at all stages, from prevention to settlement to post-conflict peacebuilding." These efforts were strengthened in 2005 with the creation of the Peace Building Commission, an office designed to coordinate all UN peacebuilding efforts.[53]

There is a similar convergence of goals and tactics in the work of Christian peace activists and scholars. During the mid-1990s, a group of Christian scholars, international relations scholars, peace activists, and conflict resolution specialists met and developed a road map of effective peacemaking practices. This group, comprised of pacifists and advocates of just war, found that despite their differences regarding the legitimacy of waging war, they agreed on the importance of constructive steps that have been used and that can be developed further in order to build peace. In *Just Peacemaking*, edited by ethicist Glen Stassen, we find an analysis of ten steps that were found to be successful in the past and worthy of further development in the future.

1. Support nonviolent direct action.
2. Take independent initiatives to reduce threat.
3. Use cooperative conflict resolution at all levels of society, from interpersonal conflicts to conflicts between peoples and nations.
4. Acknowledge responsibility for conflict and injustice and seek repentance and forgiveness.
5. Advance democracy, human rights, and religious liberty.
6. Foster just and sustainable economic development.
7. Work with emerging cooperative forces in the international system such as Regional Cooperation and Security Organizations and the UN Peacebuilding Commission.
8. Strengthen the United Nations and international efforts for cooperation and human rights (standing peacekeeping forces, International Criminal Court, and so on).

9. Reduce offensive weapons and weapons trade.
10. Encourage grassroots peacemaking groups and voluntary associations.[54]

As we continue to replace the policy of preemptive war with one of war prevention, we find ourselves in a new political world.[55] We can pursue the kind of constructive action that makes disarmament thinkable. As military intervention is successfully replaced by preventive work, nations will be able to lessen their reliance on the threat of nuclear weapons and conventional war. In this new political world, we may also find ourselves with more allies in our joint work for security and peace. Despite differences over root causes and final ends, advocates of just war and adherents of pacifism can agree on intermediate steps to prevent war—steps whose implementation requires political will, collective creativity, and sustained empathy with those we would regard as implacable foes.[56]

4

Enduring Security

We are at a fruitful moment politically, a time of fundamental reconsideration of the nature of national and international security, and of the best means to attain that security. While there is widespread support for multilateral humanitarian intervention and the responsibility to protect, there is an equally widespread disaffection with the legitimacy, morality, and even efficacy of traditional military intervention.

In the 2002 National Security Strategy of the United States, the Bush administration provided a clear articulation of a doctrine of benevolent hegemony maintained by selective multilateralism and unilateralism, one founded on unchallenged military dominance and unquestioned American exceptionalism.[1] The wisdom of this neoconservative goal and the efficacy of this strategy of unilateral military dominance are being roundly criticized from many quarters. In his most recent book, Francis Fukuyama reaffirms the neoconservative goal of "nation-building or democracy promotion" and the belief that "power—specifically American power—is often necessary to bring about moral purposes." Unlike many neoconservatives, however, he argues for "a dramatic demilitarization of American foreign policy and reemphasis on other types of policy instruments." Rather than relying exclusively on "preventive war and regime change via military intervention," he makes the case for what he calls multi-multilateralism—a vision of national and global security attained through the cooperation of a wide range of multilateral institutions, from the United Nations to NATO and the World Bank. Although he is critical of the United Nations as the sole force of multilateral cooperation, Fukuyama nonetheless states that the UN has an essential role to play in the realms of peacekeeping and in post-conflict reconstruction and peacebuilding.[2]

William Perry (U.S. secretary of defense from 1994 to 1997), Ashton Carter (member of the International and Global Affairs faculty at Harvard), and Joseph Nye Jr. (dean of Kennedy School of Government at Harvard), while also asserting the legitimacy and necessity of U.S. leadership in the world community, argue that military power alone is not enough to maintain national and international security. Perry and Carter argue for the importance of what they call preventive defense— the recognition that the U.S. best protects its interest through the use of multilateral organizations "to prevent future Cold War–scale threats to international security from emerging."[3] Nye also argues that the United States can best compel assent to its policies through the use of "soft power"—the strategic use of cultural influence and educational exchanges to create support for U.S. values and policies. He does not reject the use of "hard power," military and economic coercion, but argues for the judicious combination of both, resulting in his prescription for smart power.[4]

What is at stake in these political debates about national security and foreign policy? Not only do we

find a discussion of the utility of unilateralism or multilateralism on the feasibility and advantages of the
international rule of law and the nature of American
exceptionalism, but we also find fundamental questions
regarding the power of violence and the nature of good
and evil.

The Limits of Violence

In an August 2006 article in *The Nation*, Jonathan
Schell poses the question starkly. Given the results of
the U.S. wars in Afghanistan and Iraq, can we claim any
longer that the military power that defeats armies, kills
insurgents, and destroys buildings, monuments, and
infrastructure is a *lasting* power? Schell claims that we
may be seeing not the apotheosis but the dénouement
of empire, of economic and military security attained
through military force, and asks if the United States
"has become the fool of force and the fool of history."[5]

In 2003 William Schulz offered a trenchant critique
of imperialism:

> Empires may be born by force but they are not long sus-
> tained by it. They are sustained by a capacity to peddle
> a better idea than one's adversaries and to practice what
> you preach, to resolve conflicts equitably. . . . We knew
> that during the cold war. We knew we needed friends;
> we knew we had a better idea—democracy, freedom,
> human rights and respect for the rule of law. Debate as
> we will whether the United States today seeks empire
> and whether, if it does, that quest will be just, what
> is beyond dispute is that we have forgotten what for
> so long we knew. Moralism mixed with hubris driven
> by repression and force leads to resentment, resistance,
> and rebellion."[6]

Like Schulz, Schell points to the limits of coercive power. Drawing on Hannah Arendt's critique of totalitarianism, he claims military force is a form of weakness, a futile attempt to coerce where one cannot persuade.[7] Lest we think this merely the wishful thinking of an unregenerate advocate of nonviolence, listen to the nine "representative paradoxes of counterinsurgency" as described in a 2006 draft of *The U.S. Army and Marine Corps Counterinsurgency Field Manual*:

> The more you protect your force, the less secure you are.
> The more force is used, the less effective it is.
> The more successful counterinsurgency is, the less force that can be used and the more risk that must be accepted.
> Sometimes doing nothing is the best reaction.
> The best weapons for counterinsurgency do not shoot.
> The host nation's doing something tolerably is better than our doing it well.
> If a tactic works this week, it might not work next week; if it works in this province, it might not work in the next.
> Tactical success guarantees nothing.
> Most of the important decisions are not made by generals.[8]

Do these paradoxes mean what we think they mean? Listen to the description by Colonel Crane—the director of the Military History Institute at the Army War College and one of the writers of the new doctrine—of their genesis: "In many ways, this is a bottom-up change. . . . The young soldiers who had been through Somalia, Haiti, Bosnia, Kosovo, and now Iraq and Afghanistan, understood why we need to do this."[9] Listen, too, to a fuller explanation of some of the more startling claims:

The more force is used, the less effective it is.

Using substantial force increases the risk of collateral damage and mistakes, and increases the opportunity for insurgent propaganda.

The more successful counterinsurgency is, the less force that can be used and the more risk that must be accepted.

As the level of insurgent violence drops, the military must be used less, with stricter rules of engagement, and the police force used more.

The best weapons for counterinsurgency do not shoot.

Often dollars and ballots have more impact than bombs and bullets.

Tactical success guarantees nothing.

Military actions by themselves cannot achieve success.[10]

Sarah Sewall is currently the director of the Carr Center for Human Rights at Harvard, and former deputy assistant secretary for peacekeeping and humanitarian assistance in the Clinton administration. In her introduction to the university press edition of the *Counterinsurgency Field Manual*, she puts the work in the context of penultimate and ultimate concerns, responding to the dilemmas posed by the inability of military action to provide security against insurgents in Somalia, Afghanistan, and Iraq and "rais[ing] fundamental questions about the legitimacy, purposes, and limits of U.S. power."[11] Sewall claims that the manual reflects a rigorous application of just war theory to the conduct of counterinsurgency warfare, finally taking into account the moral, political, and tactical costs of killing noncombatants, whether those deaths be intentional or unavoidable by-products of attacks on military forces. Citing Richard Paddock, Sewall provides a telling example of such costs from the war in Iraq:

Salihee's widow, Raghad al Wazzan, said she accepted the American soldiers' presence when they first arrived in Iraq because "they came and liberated us." She sometimes helped them at the hospital where she works as a doctor. But not anymore. "Now, after they killed my husband, I hate them," she said. "I want to blow them all up."[12]

According to Sewall, the United States' current military doctrine expects and justifies significant civilian casualties at the outset of military action: "Conventional U.S. doctrine has implicitly justified collateral damage in the name of decisive victory: while overwhelming force may inadvertently harm more noncombatants initially, it ultimately serves a humanitarian purpose by ending hostilities sooner."[13]

This strategy is no longer acceptable, for a number of ethical and political reasons. Not only do civilian deaths matter, strategically and morally, but there are real limits to force, along with a corresponding need for peacebuilding activities to restore security and gain popular trust. In his foreword to the *Field Manual*, Lieutenant Colonel John Nagl states, "The nine maxims turn conventional military thinking on its head. . . . The primary goal is protecting the population," which requires sustained attention to "economic development, good governance, and the provision of essential services."[14] As Sewall states, "Securing the civilian, rather than destroying the enemy" leads to the foundational work of peacebuilding, providing "electricity, jobs and a functioning judicial system," as well as addressing the legitimate grievances that led to the insurgency.[15]

Not only are these security tasks primarily constructive, rather than reactive, but the excessive use of force—whether on the battlefield or in the interrogation and detention of detainees—is ineffective and counter-productive. The writers of the *Field Manual* state that we must remember the costs of the use of torture by the French in Algiers: The "official condoning of torture on the part of French military leadership . . . empowered the moral legitimacy of the opposition, undermined the French moral legitimacy, and caused internal fragmentation among serving officers that led to an unsuccessful coup attempt in 1962. . . . [The use of torture] contributed to their loss despite several significant military victories."[16]

The writers of the *Field Manual* pose a question of political and ethical importance, asking us to reevaluate the power of violence, honestly examining what it can and cannot accomplish. There is no doubt that violence is a powerful tool. The selective violence of the insurgency, for example, can easily disrupt peace accords and evade conventional forces. As Sewall observes, "It is far harder for the counterinsurgent to protect civilians everywhere than for the insurgent to kill them at times and places of his choosing."[17] Yet as Sewall clearly attests, to use terrorist tactics or massive force in return is not only counterproductive militarily but counterproductive ethically. Her reasoning is akin to that of Schulz. While we may indulge our "baser impulses" to stop a greater violence, she reminds us that we do so at our peril: "Counterinsurgency can bring out the worst in regular armies. . . . The insurgent's invisibility often tempts counterinsurgents to erase the all-important distinction between combatants and noncombatants . . . [or turn to a] strategy of annihilation. . . . To save ourselves, we would destroy our souls."[18]

This manual, and this debate within the U.S. military, is so very significant because it reflects a fundamental shift in understanding the power of violence. The terms of the debate are shifting: not simply a pacifist's principled rejection of a form of power recognized as efficacious but immoral, nor a just war restraint on a form of power recognized also as efficacious and necessary against dire threats. Rather, in the face of dire threats, large-scale violence is not only devastating (as the Dalai Lama says, "War is the fire and humans the kindling"[19]), but also ineffective. Military prowess alone cannot produce endurable security and lasting peace. Sewall claims that we are seeing the beginnings of a paradigm shift: the recognition that enduring security does not mean the annihilation of enemies but is only attained through the use of less force and through a greater acceptance of risk.

The prior categories so well known to political theory—neoconservativism, liberal internationalism, Jacksonian nationalism, and realism—are in flux; we are challenged to not only look again at the deadly consequences of military force, but to take seriously the limits of force to either maintain security or ensure compliance with cherished values, ideals, and institutions.

Given the limits of unilateral and multilateral force to establish enduring security, many people are exploring the concepts of integrated power and global citizenship. After the debacle of Iraq and the limits of U.S. domestic prowess in the still-unresolved economic and civic destruction in New Orleans after Hurricane Katrina, the defense of American exceptionalism sounds as hollow and anachronistic as a defense of the divine right of kings.

Many scholars, activists, and government officials are exploring the implications of a new paradigm: a shift from seeing the United States as the undisputed leader of an international system—with moral legitimacy and military and economic might—to seeing the

U.S. as a responsible partner, a member of a global community in which others may lead where we cannot, and
where we have much to learn from other nations and
other peoples. In an interdependent world, our security
is best attained through cooperation with others, and
not through unilateral military action. Richard Leone
(president of the Century Foundation) and John Podesta (president of the Center for American Progress),
in the foreword to the papers presented at their jointly
sponsored conference "Power and Superpower: Global
Leadership in the 21st Century," made the following
observation:

> The safety and prosperity of the American people
> depend on the complex and abiding links that connect
> our country to its partners around the world. Events
> in other lands increasingly impact the American home-
> land: pollution crosses oceans, diseases do not stop at
> customs posts, and suicide bombers are not deterred by
> military action.

> We have learned . . . that deployment of our military
> power is not the answer to every problem.[20]

Religion and Violence

Given how easily even the most comprehensive peace
accords may be disrupted and how recalcitrant are the
economic and political sources of social unrest, what
sense does it make to speak of enduring security and
sustainable peace? Can we find in our religious traditions resources that enable us to acknowledge our
responsibility, power, and limits with both audacity and
humility? The recognition of limits and the proclivity to
abuse power can be paralyzing. If even our best actions

are tainted with self-interest or subject to unpredictable consequences, why act at all? If we have no guarantee that our best efforts at sustainable peace will not do more harm than good, how can we move forward with foresight and responsibility?

Here our religious and ethical traditions offer ways of living in light of ambiguity and loss. Let us turn to the words of two great proponents of nonviolence, Mahatma Gandhi and the Trappist monk Thomas Merton, respectively.

> The law of love will work, just as the law of gravitation will work, whether we accept it or not. Just as a scientist will work wonders out of various applications of the law of nature, even so a man who applies the law of love with scientific precision can work greater wonders. . . . Only our explorations have not gone far enough and so it is not possible for everyone to see all its workings. Such, at any rate, is the hallucination, if it is one, under which I am laboring. The more I work at this law the more I feel the delight in life, the delight in the scheme of the universe. It gives me a peace and a meaning of the mysteries of nature that I have no power to describe.[21]

> There can be no question that unless war is abolished the world will remain constantly in a state of madness and desperation in which, because of the immense destructive power of modern weapons, the danger of catastrophe will be imminent. . . . Christians must become active in every possible way, mobilizing all their resources for the fight against war. . . . Peace is to be preached, nonviolence is to be explained as a practical method, and not left to be mocked as an outlet for crackpots who want to make a show of themselves.

Prayer and sacrifice must be used as the most effective spiritual weapons in the war against war, and like all weapons they must be used with deliberate aim: not just with a vague aspiration for peace and security, but against violence and against war.[22]

Drawing from the wisdom of the religious traditions of humanity—Gandhi from Hinduism and Christianity, Merton from Christianity and Buddhism—each of these leaders clearly saw the horror and futility of war, yet also recognized the possibility, and the necessity, of nonviolent responses to injustice, fear, and oppression.

Although these quotations are familiar to many of us, I wish to highlight an often-overlooked aspect of each. Why does Gandhi speak of "scientific precision"? What does Merton mean with his warning about nonviolence as "an outlet for crackpots who want to make a show of themselves," or his comment about "a vague aspiration for peace and security"? What would it mean to follow Merton's injunction and use spiritual weapons with "deliberate aim"? Although certain of the ultimate power of love and the ability of goodness to prevail over evil, Gandhi and Merton were well aware that our attempts to live out that love could be ineffective. They encouraged activists to craft nonviolent forms of witness and noncooperation with injustice that were geared to the nuances of the situation at hand, reflecting and evoking the best of a particular people at a specific time. This sensibility is carried forward in all those committed to strategic peacebuilding who encourage us to use the best of technical rationality in the service of moral aims: assessing the efficacy and impact of our efforts to reconcile deep-seated conflicts, to reintegrate former combatants, to heal victims of rape and dislocation, to reform judicial systems, and to create equitable and sustainable economic systems.

Many proponents of nonviolence maintain a faith in the inevitable triumph of justice. For instance, Martin Luther King Jr. often cited the words of the abolitionist minister Theodore Parker: "The arc of the universe may be long, but it bends toward justice."[23] Gandhi is another example: he was as forthcoming in acknowledging that his efforts at nonviolence were experiments—and thus subject to failure—as he was confident that ultimately nonviolence would prevail. The mission statement of the American Friends Service Committee expresses a conviction shared by many Christian pacifists:

> We nurture the faith that conflicts can be resolved nonviolently, that enmity can be transformed into friendship, strife into cooperation, poverty into well-being, and injustice into dignity and participation. We believe that ultimately goodness can prevail over evil, and oppression in all its many forms can give way.[24]

Good and Evil

What about those of us, however, who do not share Gandhi and King's certainty about the triumph of good over evil? Despite our best efforts, and those of our community and friends, many of us have no idea if our own children will grow into ethically responsible, productive, and resilient adults. We hardly have confidence in our ability to chart the trajectory of the entirety of human history.

Even without knowledge of the cumulative or ultimate meaning of human affairs, it is possible to find resilience in the face of what could be paralyzing ambiguity in the face of the struggle between violence and nonviolence, justice and exploitation, good and evil. This is, as William Schulz noted, a long-explored issue within religious traditions. He asks, "[What is] the role of religious values and institutions[?] Should they hold up ideals in order to advance the highly honorable tradition of speaking truth to power, even when those ideals have little practical chance of being adopted and power cannot hear? Or should they sully their hands with the hard choices of policymaking, knowing that they may thereby compromise their claims to unblemished moral authority?" If we choose to follow, with Schulz, the second choice, plumbing the depths of ambiguity and responsibility, I suggest we can learn from two traditions, finding a compelling logic of good and evil that may offer direction and hope. These traditions grapple with the dilemma of Christian folly posed so clearly by Dietrich Bonhoeffer: capitulation in the face of overweening power and the fear of moral ambiguity.[25]

Let us consider a set of stories and a type of practice that can enable creativity and wonder in the face of such moral complexity—wisdom drawn from the work of Vietnamese and Japanese Buddhists—and from Native American writers and activists. Both these traditions, borne by cultures that the U.S. tried to defeat, militarily and culturally, offer resources for a transformed political and ethical imagination—one in which we forgo both the illusion of a security based on the triumph of righteousness and the annihilation of enemies, and a peace predicated on the absence of conflict and injustice.

In *The Truth about Stories*, noted Canadian author Thomas King points to the possibility of a new story emerging about our collective identity as indigenous Americans and as Euro-Americans. King recounts the power of story, citing authors from Leslie Marmon Silko to Gerald Vizenor and Diane Clancy, all who would subscribe to King's observation that the truth about stories is that that's all we are. The Okanagan storyteller Jeannette Armstrong tells us that "through my language I understand I am being spoken to, I'm not the one speaking. The words are coming from many tongues and mouths of Okanagan people and the land around them. I am a listener to the language's stories, and when my words form I am merely retelling the same stories in different patterns."[26]

Those colonized by the United States have long carried the stories of the cruelty and barbarism unleashed by imperial power. Thomas King provides a cogent example and response:

Indians, it seemed, could offer little inspiration or example to civilized humans, and colonists saw little need to examine either the Indian or Indian culture. . . . Jonas Johannis Michaluis, in a letter to the Reverend Adrianus Smoutuis, summed up the feelings that most colonists had for Indians when he described them as "savage and wild, strangers to all decency, yea, and uncivil and stupid as garden poles." "Stupid as garden poles." It's funny, isn't it? And a little annoying, too. But there's no point in being angry. These are just the sounds and smell of empire—fear, racism, greed, arrogance."[27]

Given the cost of imperial power, King asks us to consider a fundamental shift in the ends of political and ethical action. He paints a vivid picture of the story of the West: "If we had to have a patron story for North America, we could do worse than the one about Alexander the Great, who, when faced with the puzzle of the Gordian knot, solved that problem with nothing more than a strong arm and a sharp sword."[28] King juxtaposes this Western story of decisive force with another story, deeply held within many Native American traditions and, according to King, overlooked even by sympathetic Euro-American readers and interpreters. King states that many of us have seen the communal ethos and relation to land so central to indigenous life, but have missed the equally fundamental claim that the greatest folly is any attempt to destroy evil.[29] Leslie Marmon Silko, in her elegiac novel *Ceremony*, recounts the story of our militarized world and its immense powers of destruction, powers held at bay only as people refuse to destroy the destroyers.[30] King explains the significance of Silko's stance:

> But what Momaday and other Native writers suggest is that there are other ways of imagining the world, ways that do not depend so much on oppositions as they do on cooperations, and they raise the tantalizing question of what else one might do if confronted with the appearance of evil. So just how would we manage a universe in which the attempt to destroy evil is seen as a form of insanity?[31]

This question, of wise rather than foolhardy responses to widespread and intractable evil, while important individually and spiritually, is also being refracted in debates over human security and the "responsibility to protect" peoples from genocide and civil war.

What a situation we have—a lively, growing advocacy of human security and strategic peacebuilding but without guarantees of either triumph or virtue. How do we take steps to stop brutality and crimes against humanity when we recognize that evil is not solely within them, but also within us? How do we maintain presence, creativity, *and* openness to our own responsibility and fallibility?

In thinking through such puzzles, I have found the work of Michael Hogue to be extremely helpful. What Hogue finds in the moral challenges of climate change has deep resonance with the moral and theological challenges of building peace. Like those addressing the crisis of climate change, we face "problems that are global in scale, intergenerational in reach, and carried by institutions whose temporal frame of reference is immediate and short term."[32]

Furthermore, the ambiguity of global and intergenerational change is exacerbated by what Hogue finds in the realm of ordinary personal and interpersonal life:

> You may have noticed, as I have, that life can be a tricky business. . . . The life of the body is one of illness and health, of eating and sleeping and loving and mourning. The life of the mind is one of perplexity and discovery and awakening, and for some of us, of forgetting. And then there is the fact that all of this human trickiness, the joy and sorrow, is experienced within a broader world that is full to brimming with others who are also engaged in the business of getting by, getting along, making the best of things, and seeking the good and the right. . . . It is a wonderful thing that no one of us is an island unto ourselves. And yet this fact also means that our lives are ones of constant negotiation, compromise, and complex relations.[33]

It is easy to avoid ambiguity and seek solace in definitive social critiques and simple political solutions. Might we find, though, a symbolic wonder, engagement, and desire that delights in the play of paradox, anticipates the challenge of unintended consequences, and embraces the requisite humility of being a species marked by fallibility and error?

Knowing and Nonknowing

Many voices are pointing the way to such an understanding of the terrible sweetness of life. Let us explore
the ethically and politically evocative insights found in
the work of contemporary Engaged Buddhists, with a
focus on three elements that foster the practice of skillful means in the pursuit of just peace: the nondualism
of good and evil; emptiness, or *sunyata*, as pregnancy;
and the interplay of knowing and nonknowing.

The Buddhist tradition is rich, complex, and in a process of continuing change and development. I am drawing on a particular strand of this immensely variegated
tradition, one that addresses Western traditions from
the point of view of being itself influenced by those
same traditions. Just as Buddhism has taken different
forms in the past, transformed as it has moved from
India to China, Tibet, and Japan, so, too, the Buddhist
engagement with Western modernity and humanism
is leading to another manifestation of Buddhist practice, one focused on political institutions, social justice,
and political transformation.[34] Masao Abe, a leading
exponent of Zen to the West, makes a clear distinction
between these newly emerging forms of social engagement and the practices of traditional Buddhism. Abe
claims that one finds, with only a few exceptions, "an
indifference to social evil in the history of Buddhism."
He states that the focus in most of Buddhist history,
even within the Bodhisattva vow "to save all beings,"
has not been "society at large" but other individuals.
He states that he has learned from Christian liberation
theology that the Buddhist focus on "interrelationality
and compassion . . . may serve to cover social inequality and injustice."[35] The leading advocates of Engaged
Buddhism, Thich Nhat Hanh and Sulak Sivaraksa, are

themselves engaged in intense dialogue and interactions with Western traditions of the support of human rights, the equality of women, and work for social and environmental justice.[36]

Engaged Buddhism is itself a contested term, described by some as a fourth yana, or turning of the wheel of the dharma.[37] Other scholars and Buddhist practitioners, however, warn of the dangers in this terminology. Stephen Batchelor, for example, claims that the term is a misleading tautology, detaching action from other aspects of Buddhist practice. He describes insight and compassionate response as "two wings of a bird" and states that "authentic Buddhist practice necessarily leads to . . . engagement with the world."[38]

It is the insights and critiques of this contested and evolving tradition that I have found helpful in addressing the political challenges of establishing sustainable security and enduring peace. Buddhism, or dharma practice, is not a set of beliefs but a course of action, ways of practice that create or evoke "contentment with joy, and equanimity in the face of suffering." These nondualistic ways of experiencing good and evil, self and others, provide a distinct way of holding suffering, anger, and fear, and a distinct way of imagining and engaging in creative political action.[39]

Masao Abe offers a clear challenge to both Buddhist individualism and Western triumphalism: "Buddhism tends to put priority on enlightenment over practice and thereby threatens to become quietism. Conversely, Christianity tends to put priority on action over prayer and threatens to become a crusade."[40]

The appeal of the crusade is clear—it is the challenge of establishing the secure reign of righteousness and justice by the ultimate defeat of unmitigated and irredeemable evil. Why, however, would anyone think that such a project is remotely feasible? At the core of triumphalism and righteous violence is the conviction of a clear divide between good and evil, oppressor and oppressed, just and unjust. Although we are now inundated with such rhetoric from the neoconservative defense of American exceptionalism, this rhetoric knows no political or religious bounds. Brian Victoria found such rhetoric in the Buddhist justification of Japanese imperialism and military conquest during World War II.[41] And, I must admit, the rhetoric of self-righteous certainty can also be found among leftists and progressives.

Abe reminds us that a stark division between good and evil fails to acknowledge our embeddedness in an interdependent world. Let us explore more fully the impact of his challenging statement: "It is not that we have a dilemma of good and evil but that we are the dilemma of good and evil." Abe states that as we become deeply aware of the extent of human suffering, and as we are honest about the difficulties of our own struggle to live with compassion and integrity, we realize that "[the] priority of good over evil is an ethical imperative but not an actual human situation. In human beings good and evil have equal power. I cannot say that my good is stronger than my evil although I should try to overcome my evil by my good."[42]

This realization of the equal power of good and evil, even within ourselves, does not diminish the ethical imperative of choosing good over evil, but recasts it. Abe makes a claim that is startling to Western ears: "Ethically speaking, Buddhists clearly realize that good should conquer evil. However, through the experience of their inner struggle, Buddhists cannot say that good is strong enough to overcome evil. Good and evil are completely antagonistic principles, resisting each other with equal force, yet inseparably connected and displaying an existential antinomy as a whole."[43]

Given this connection of good and evil, the goal of action is not defeating evil but learning how to act in light of the power and connection of both good and evil. As Abe explains, "In Buddhism, what is essential for salvation is not to overcome evil with good, . . . but to be emancipated from the existential antinomy of good and evil and to awaken to Emptiness prior to the opposition between good and evil."[44]

It is here that we may find another contribution of Engaged Buddhists to an understanding of the dynamics of political engagement, a recognition of the fluid ambiguity and creative power of emptiness. Drawing on the poetry of Nagarjuna, a philosopher monk who lived in India during the second century, Stephen Batchelor describes emptiness as "a condition in which one aspires to live," a freeing immersion in the "the sublime contingency of self and things."[45]

Many contemporary Buddhists follow the work of Nagarjuna and his evocation of the unfathomable and unpredictable interconnectedness that characterizes all existence. Ken Jones claims that a core connotation of emptiness is lost in many Western interpretations. Emptiness does not connote nothingness or nihilism, because, he explains, the Sanskrit term *shunyata* "also carries the meaning of swollen, or pregnant—and [emptiness] is indeed pregnant with the potentiality of liberative, energizing creativity."[46] Each situation is intrinsically fluid, pregnant with multiple and unpredictable possibilities. Good and ill may emerge from the same action. Our commitment to justice and peace through the exercise of skillful means may lead in directions and result in consequences we can neither predict nor control. Abe acknowledges that the recognition of the unpredictability and contingency of emptiness can evoke quiescence.[47] Buddhist teacher Pema Chodron states that it can lead to rigidity and denial.[48] Batchelor, however, attests that our honest recognition of the pregnancy of each moment may also evoke joyful audacity.[49]

Now to a third dimension of Buddhist practice and its implications for political action. The focus on skillful means by the practitioners of Engaged Buddhism may sound as though reformers know what is best for society and are using the "liberative arts" to bring others to our insights. This misses, however, what is most challenging about Engaged Buddhism, the freedom and honesty of a genuine acceptance of the limits of our knowledge and of the possibility of the new.[50]

Thich Nhat Hanh says that the avoidance of dogmatism, expressed in the first of the fourteen mindfulness trainings, is "the roar of lion. Its spirit is characteristic of Buddhism."

> *Aware of the suffering created by fanaticism and intolerance,* we are determined not to be idolatrous about or bound to any doctrine, theory or ideology, even Buddhist ones. *Aware of the suffering brought about when we impose our views on others,* we are committed not to force others, even our children, by any means whatsoever—such as authority, threat, money, propaganda, or indoctrination—to adopt our views.[51]

Within the work of Engaged Buddhists we find a form of action founded on both knowing and nonknowing: *knowing,* from the best of all we are, can see, and can think about a situation, yet offering that knowledge as a gift, open to the transformation of insight and analysis in light of the gifts of others and the surprising and unpredictable consequences of our wholehearted attempts to live justly.

In this discussion of Engaged Buddhism, I am following the approach described by Kenneth Kraft and Stephanie Kaza in *Dharma Rain*. They do not claim that Buddhism is the solution to the ecological crisis, but present, rather, the ways in which Buddhism, along with other philosophical and religious traditions, may be a catalyst for a healing response to the severe challenges of ecological degradation.[52] What would it mean if the goal of our actions were not the eradication of evil, but a catalytic response to the evil of ourselves and others? I am not imagining what social and political life might be if everyone were enlightened. Rather, I am exploring dharma practice as a self-critical and creative means of working together, knowing that we are neither fully awake nor wholly compassionate.

I speak with those peacemakers who are acknowledging that we really do not know how to bring peace, reconciliation, and justice. The solutions that seemed so promising in theory prove to be surprisingly complex and ambiguous in actuality. We remain, however, committed to the art of living for peace and justice for all beings even as we admit that we do not know how to bring a measure of peace and justice in a world of *dukka*—a world of suffering shaped by the three poisons of greed, ill will, and delusion. We are learning how to work for justice in this world, a world in which we can readily see the fixations of other individuals, peoples, and nations—a world in which we may, if we are honest and aware, even catch a glimpse of our own constitutive delusions.

I see our challenge to be knowing that we are as likely as our "opponents" to succumb to delusion, greed, and ill will—and finding, therefore, ways of shaping our institutions and our political and spiritual practices to reflect this knowledge, to provide checks from others that we cannot fully provide for ourselves. Here the task of cultivated awareness becomes a social task as well as an individual discipline.

Buddhist traditions offer much in the way of nurturing individual openness to the acceptance of emptiness through rich and varied traditions of meditation that evoke sustained awareness of the passing flux of life. The Western philosophical and political tradition has, however, something to offer at this point. Let us apply a Kantian perspective to Buddhist ethics. According to Kant, the work of a well-governed state is that it enables its citizens to be moral. Kant saw this in the support given by the state for the exercise of human freedom and reason.[53] To our calculus of moral accountability, let us add mindfulness of the pregnant emptiness of each interaction, and mindfulness of the nondualism of good and evil. Such mindfulness can be fostered in a number of ways: by providing the institutional time and space for reflection, awareness, and critique, and through regularized means of eliciting and evaluating dissent and critique. A well-governed society would recount the dangerous memories of cruelty and complicity not only of others, but of ourselves, holding these memories as part of the story of who we are—as individuals, as an organization, as a political party, and as a people. We can learn as much from our stories of failure as from our stories of triumph.[54]

At the core of this third way of peacemaking is a view of human nature and of human possibilities that is different from either Niebuhrian and Augustinian realism or philosophical and religious aspirations for a new humanity. Advocates of Augustinian and Niebuhrian realism claim that, given human sinfulness, violence is required to contain and constrain the worst of human behavior. Within more idealistic and utopian views—whether Christian, Buddhist, or socialist—we find a very different claim: the world will be at peace when all people are enlightened, transformed, or freed from the constraints of injustice.

The third way of peacebuilding accepts part of each perspective and challenges others. With Augustine and Niebuhr we grant the depth and ubiquity of human depravity yet find that violence is neither checked nor defeated by violence alone. While there may be a role for force, it is certainly less than has been accepted within just war tenets to date. The recent *Counterinsurgency Field Manual* reflects this awareness, gained on the ground, of how what is intended as decisive violence may often exacerbate and prolong armed conflict and civil unrest. A mixture of economic, diplomatic, humanitarian, and military initiatives is far more likely to stop armed conflict and prevent the outbreak of further conflicts in the future.

While Christian and Buddhist traditions have long advocated such forms of "smart power," appealing to human desires for cooperation, safety, and mutual well-being, many of their hopes have also focused on a transformed, enlightened humanity. What if we gave this assumption a twist, akin to Batchelor's understanding of enlightenment? To be enlightened may be to recognize that we are not enlightened, nor are others, and yet to choose to work for peace in this world, seeing and responding to the proclivity for domination and violence not just in others, but in ourselves.

This approach to peacemaking has a long lineage. Jonathan Dean—cofounder of Global Action to Prevent War and former U.S. ambassador who worked with Soviet president Mikhail Gorbachev on disarmament—grounds our contemporary efforts to build peace and security in a process that accelerated for the United States and Europe only two hundred years ago:

> The convulsions of the Napoleonic Wars also led in the United Kingdom, Western Europe and the United States to another important new phenomenon in the history of war—groups of public citizens, some of them quite large, organized regionally and often nationally in opposition to war. . . . What happened here, after acceptance of war over millennia as desirable or at least as a given component of human history, was deliberate, conscious rejection of war as such. . . . This development marked a revolution in human affairs and in the history of war and peace.[55]

These efforts reflect another trend in European political thought—the concern with the rule of law, both within and between states, and lawful arbitration, rather than war, as a means of resolving internal and external disputes. Rather than expect or seek a fundamental change in human nature, or rely on moral or religious critiques of war, "the peace societies ultimately gave priority to mechanisms and measures to constrain war over intellectual arguments to end war, believing that practical measures would convince more people than abstract argument."[56]

Nondualism of Good and Evil

How do we act if we acknowledge that evil is as much within us, the undoubted bearers of virtue, as it is within our more benighted opponents? How do we act if we also acknowledge the equal power of good and evil? Or, to be more precise, how do we act if we acknowledge the equal but differential power of good and evil? Just as evil and force can readily destroy a social order, yet cannot establish a lasting peace, the good so patiently achieved can readily be undone—not only by cruelty, resentment, and fear, but by the dual temptations of undue self-satisfaction and the unwitting imposition of yesterday's solutions on today's challenges.

Those of us who are working for peace are not a righteous vanguard. We can, and will, abuse cooperative power and need our own Trickster stories to remind us of our flaws and excesses. There is no multitude, no group any less likely than others to abuse power—as the political philosopher Frantz Fanon knew well, and as revolutionaries of all sorts forget to our peril. Wisdom, ongoing self-critique, and accountability are required of *all* of us, not just the imperial others, in the exercise of social, cultural, economic, and political power.

What are transformative metaphors for compassionate, self-critical, and creative engagement when our goal is neither the ultimate defeat of evil nor fundamental and permanent social change? It is simply (but significantly?) a less destructive way of playing who and what we are. Rather than solving all problems forever, for all people, and for all times, we have the challenge of living with integrity *now* and of teaching, mentoring, and nurturing future generations who will face unanticipated challenges, in addition to the perennial ones of growing in courage, justice, and fairness. What image can hold these strands of fallibility and interdependence, of companionship, unresolved tensions, and ongoing risk? Our goal now, to use the words of Foucault, is an experimentation with technologies of the self that enable us to use power creatively and self-critically.[57] If we seek to use power truthfully, our goal is not a final or universal resolution to injustice, but rather actions that manifest accountability and creativity.

We are accountable to those whose lives are destroyed by violence; we are accountable as well to those who find our nonviolent strategies unpersuasive and dangerously naïve. How do we respond to the use of military force by political leaders and the inability of the critics of war to decisively reject such force? Rather than merely denounce these responses, we need to understand them more deeply. People respond to danger with the tools that they have. While we may be able to imagine alternative responses—the use of international mediators, an international court, and so forth—these responses do not have the known status and evident power of military force. The International Criminal Court, a plausible venue for prosecuting terrorists, has only recently been ratified, and it does not have a solid history or widespread acceptance. By continuing to rely on military force, nations are responding with the institutions and the means that they have, know, and trust. Furthermore, for many people, "real" power—whether human or divine—is expressed in the decisive defeat of enemies, not in mutual transformation, healing, and reconciliation.

In the face of grave threats, war, with all of its costs, is still the preferred option, and forms of nonviolent action and conflict resolution and prevention are seen quite baldly as "doing nothing" or as appeasing dangerous enemies. The successes of the civil rights movement and Gandhi's nonviolent campaigns are thought to be unique, dependent on the beneficence of the British and

U.S. citizenry, and not indicative of the response to be expected from implacable enemies.

A further challenge to persuasively conveying alternatives to war concerns our own actions and behaviors. Just as many of our conservative colleagues suspect that we underestimate the perfidy and resolve of those perceived as enemies, so they suppose that we overestimate the virtue and competence of peace activists and peacekeepers. These fears are not misplaced.

Security may come, paradoxically, from our openness to fragility—from seeing the ways peace can be and is undermined, from recognizing the limits and unintended consequences of our actions and remaining vital, engaged, and creative. Like the audacious beauty of the finest jazz performances, we may become virtuosos of life: playing insights and failures, evoking and nurturing as much beauty and justice as can be created for this time and at this place. Here our aspirations are modest, and again Foucault is instructive. Our work does not have the import of some decisive turn or grand shift in human affairs, but rather we are simply doing our best, providing resources, and creating the matrix for others to respond to challenges that we can neither imagine nor forestall.[58]

Within this third wave of constructive and self-critical political organizing, the fundamental gesture is not so much the prophetic "turn and repent" as it is the aesthetic imperative: See!

See what surrounds us, shapes us, and sustains us.

See the costs, the contours of pain and suffering, the tragedies caused by fear, isolation, and arrogance.

See also the contours of possibility, the resources of insight, courage, and goodwill.

See who we are, in all our moral complexity and culpability.

As we acknowledge our constitutive limits, as we see the manifold possibilities that surround us, let us shape together a politics of honesty and hope, an aesthetic pragmatism that embraces the challenges of the present with virtuosity, wonder, and joy.

Notes

Foreword

1. See Victor Nell, "Cruelty's Rewards: The Gratifications of Perpetrators and Spectators," forthcoming in *Behavioral and Brain Sciences*, www.bbsonline.org (2005).

2. Quoted in Helene Poulet, "We Were Calling to Death," *Harper's Magazine*, February 2003, 14–15.

Introduction

1. Fatalities as of August 8, 2008, 10:00 a.m. EDT. Statistics found on the official Web site of the U.S. Department of Defense, which monitors the U.S. casualty status of the war in Iraq. Accessed online at http://www.defenselink.mil/news/casualty.pdf.

2. Michel Foucault, in an interview for *Le Monde* conducted on April 6–7, 1980, by Christian Delacampagne. Foucault opted to interview under anonymity, going by "The Masked Philosopher." Interview reprinted in Michel Foucault, *Ethics: Subjectivity and Truth*, Essential Works of Foucault (1954–1984), vol. 1, ed. Paul Rabinow (New York: New Press, 1997), 323.

3. Adam Hochschild, *Bury the Chains: Prophets and Rebels in the Fight to Free an Empire's Slaves* (Boston: Houghton Mifflin, 2005).

4. Bill Keller, "Joe Slovo, Anti-Apartheid Stalinist, Dies at 68," *New York Times*, January 7, 1995.

5. Ernesto Che Guevara, *The Motorcycle Diaries* (Koln: Kiepenheuer & Witsch, 2004); Ernesto Che Guevara, *The Complete Bolivian Diaries of Che Guevara and Other Captured Documents*, ed. Daniel James (New York: Stein and Day, 1968).

6. J. K. Gibson-Graham, *A Postcapitalist Politics* (Minneapolis: University of Minnesota Press, 2006), 79–80.

7. Ibid., 88.

8. Ibid., 159.

9. Glen Stassen, ed., *Just Peacemaking: Ten Practices for Abolishing War*, 2nd ed. (Cleveland: Pilgrim, 2004); Lisa Schirch, *The Little Book of Strategic Peacebuilding* (Intercourse, Pa.: Good Books, 2006).

10. Kofi Annan, cited by Sir Brian Urquhart, preface to *A United Nations Emergency Peace Service: To Prevent Genocide and Crimes against Humanity*, ed. Robert Johansen (New York: Global Action to Prevent War, Nuclear Age Peace Foundation, and World Federalist Movement, 2006), 9.

11. Robert C. Johansen, "The United Nations Emergency Peace Service: Executive Summary," in *A United Nations Emergency Peace Service: to Prevent Genocide and Crimes against Humanity*, ed. Robert Johansen (New York: Global Action to Prevent War, Nuclear Age Peace Foundation, and World Federalist Movement, 2006), 22.

12. Schirch, *Strategic Peacebuilding.*

13. Ibid., 26.

14. Catherine Barnes, "Weaving the Web: Civil-Society Roles in Working with Conflict and Building Peace," in *People Building Peace II: Successful Stories of Civil Society*, ed. Paul van Tongeren, Malin Brenk, Marte Hellema, and Juliette Verhoeven (Boulder: Lynne Rienner, 2005), 21–22.

15. Schirch, *Strategic Peacebuilding*, 33, 67.

16. M. K. Gandhi, *Non-violent Resistance (Satyagraha)* (New York: Schocken, 1951), 275; Martin Luther King Jr., "An Experiment in Love," in *A Testament of Hope: The Essential Writings of Martin Luther King, Jr.*, ed. James M. Washington (Cambridge, Mass.: Harper & Row, 1986), 18.

17. Vern Redekop, *From Violence to Blessing: How an Understanding of Deep-Rooted Conflict Can Open Paths of Reconciliation* (Ottawa: Novalis, 2002), 51.

1. Peacekeeping

1. William F. Schulz, *In Our Own Best Interest: How Defending Human Rights Benefits Us All* (Boston: Beacon, 2002).

2. Leonard Kapungu, "Peacekeeping, Peacebuilding and the Lessons-Learned Process," in *Peacebuilding: A Field Guide*, ed. Luc Reychler and Thania Paffenholz (Boulder: Lynne Rienner, 2001), 436. See also Kofi Annan's message for the 2004 International Day of United Nations Peacekeepers. Full text found in the May 24, 2004, United Nations press release "Peacekeeping Missions Best Way of Ensuring Sustainable Peace, Says Secretary-General on International Day of UN Peacekeepers," online at http://www.un.org/News/Press/docs/2004/sgsm9321.doc.htm (July 15, 2008).

3. Kapungu, "Peacekeeping, Peacebuilding," 435. See also Michael W. Doyle and Nicholas Sambanis, *Making War and Building Peace: United Nations Peace Operations* (Princeton: Princeton University Press, 2006).

4. Doyle and Sambanis, *Making War and Building Peace*, 12–14.

5. Sir Brian Urquhart, preface to *A United Nations Emergency Peace Service: To Prevent Genocide and Crimes against Humanity*, ed. Robert Johansen (New York: Global Action to Prevent War, Nuclear Age Peace Foundation, and World Federalist Movement, 2006), 7.

6. Doyle and Sambanis, *Making War and Building Peace*, 14–15.

7. Ibid., 15–18.

8. Ibid., 161–71, 289–302.

9. Ibid., 18.

10. Julia Fitzpatrick, "From 'Never Again' to Responsibility to Protect," *Global Solutions Quarterly* (Summer 2007): 4.

11. Kapungu, "Peacekeeping, Peacebuilding," 435.

12. International Commission on Intervention and State Sovereignty, *The Responsibility to Protect: Report of the International Commission on Intervention and State Sovereignty* (Ottawa: International Development Research Centre, 2001), 5–6.

13. Ibid.

14. Ibid., 6.

15. Ibid., 12: 1.19.

16. Ibid., 34: 4.19.

17. Ibid., 36: 4.29.

18. Ibid., 35: 4.25–26.

19. Ibid., 17: 2.1.

20. Ibid., 13: 1.20.

21. Ibid., 63: 8.15.

22. Ibid., 63: 8.16.

23. Ibid., 63: 8.13.

24. From a conversation with William Schulz, former executive director of Amnesty International, USA, January 24, 2008.

25. STAND, online at www.standnow.org; Save Darfur, online at www.savedarfur.org (July 15, 2008).

26. H. Peter Langille, *Bridging the Commitment-Capacity Gap* (New York: Center for UN Reform Education, 2002).

27. Quoted on p. 9 of United Nations Emergency Peace Service proposal. Proposal examined at symposium entitled "To Prevent Genocide and Crimes against Humanity: Diverse Perspectives on a Standing, Rapid-Reaction UN Emergency Peace Service," sponsored by the Global Action to Prevent War, the Rutgers Global Legal Studies Program, and the International Law Society, held at the Rutgers School of Law in Newark March 29, 2007.

28. International Commission on Intervention and State Sovereignty, *Responsibility to Protect*, 51: 7.1.

29. Ibid., 40: 5.8.

30. Schirch, *Strategic Peacebuilding*, 35–39, 76.

31. Catherine A. Mullhaupt and Jean Hughes Raber, "Community Policing Helps Townships Tackle Crime," National Center for Community Policing, Michigan State University, online at http://www.cj.mus.edu/~people/cp/mta.html (December 15, 2007).

32. Oxfam Australia and Oxfam New Zealand, "Bridging the Gap between State and Society: New Directions for Solomon Islands," Human Security Report Project newsletter (August 2006).

33. Ikechi Mgbeoji, *Collective Insecurity: The Liberian Crisis, Unilateralism, and Global Order* (Vancouver: UBC, 2003), 104. Citing Philip Gourevitch, "The Triumph of Evil" (interview), Public Broadcasting System, online at http://www.pbs.org/wgbh/pages/frontline/shows/evil/interviews/gourevitch.html (May 4, 2002).

34. International Commission on Intervention and State Sovereignty, *Responsibility to Protect*, 37: 4.35.

35. Richard Falk, "Humanitarian Intervention: Imperatives and Problematics," in *Human Rights in the World Community: Issues and Action*, 3rd ed., ed. Richard Pierre Claude and Burns H. Weston (Philadelphia: University of Pennsylvania Press, 2006), 401, 406.

36. International Commission on Intervention and State Sovereignty, *Responsibility to Protect*, 16: 1.39–41; 22: 2.28–29; 23: 2.33.

37. *Human Security Report 2005: War and Peace in the 21st Century* (New York: Oxford University Press, 2005), 28.

38. International Commission on Intervention and State Sovereignty, *Responsibility to Protect*, 33: 4.12.

39. Ibid., 13: 1.22.

40. David R. Gushee, *The Righteous Gentiles of the Holocaust: A Christian Interpretation* (Minneapolis: Fortress Press, 1994), chs. 2–3.

41. Thomas G. Weiss and Don Hubert, *Responsibility to Protect: Research, Bibliography, Background*, supplementary volume to the report of the International Commission on Intervention and State Sovereignty (Ottawa: International Development Research Centre, 2007), 146.

42. Tony Blair, quoted in CNN article entitled "Photos Allege Abuse of Iraqis by British Troops" (May 1, 2004), online at http://edition.cnn.com/2004/WORLD/meast/04/30/iraq.brit.prisoner.abuse/ (July 15, 2008).

43. Albert Bandura, "Moral Disengagement in the Perpetration of Inhumanities," *Personality and Social Psychology Review*, special issue on evil and violence (1999), 3, 193–209. The quote by Gonzales is not noted by Bandura but may be found in the transcript of the Amy Goodman show, *Democracy*

Now! from July 1, 2005, online at www.democracynow.org/
article.pl?sid=05/01/07/1621235 (July 15, 2008).

44. Bandura, "Moral Disengagement," 25–26.

45. Ibid., 27.

46. Ibid., 9.

47. Ibid., 28–29.

48. Ibid., 30. William Schulz, intro. to ch. 7, reading 10, in
The Phenomenon of Torture: Readings and Commentary, ed.
William F. Schulz (Philadelphia: University of Pennsylvania
Press, 2007), 347; Marc DuBois, "Training and Education," in
Schulz, *Phenomenon of Torture*, 350.

49. International Commission on Intervention and State
Sovereignty, *Responsibility to Protect*, 36: 4.32.

50. Ibid., 37: 4.33; 38: 4.39.

51. Don Kraus, CEO of Citizens for Global Solutions, on
the June 11, 2007, letter in support of House Resolution 213
calling for the establishment of a United Nations Emergency
Peace Service. Online at http://www.globalsolutions.org/in_
the_news/u_s_congress_urged_support_permanent_un_force
(September 15, 2008).

52. Friends Committee on National Legislation, *Peaceful
Prevention of Deadly Conflict: If War Is Not the Answer, What
Is?* (Washington, D.C.: FCNL Education Fund, 2005), 8.

53. Read more about Religions for Peace online at http://
www.rfpusa.org/ (July 15, 2008).

54. The Dalai Lama, *Ethics for the New Millennium* (New
York: Riverhead, 1999), 212.

55. Ibid., 212–13. For more on an Engaged Buddhist
approach to peacemaking, peacebuilding, and peacekeeping,
see also Sulak Sivaraksa, *Conflict, Culture, Change: Engaged
Buddhism in a Globalizing World* (Boston: Wisdom, 2005).

2. Peacemaking

1. Michael W. Doyle and Nicholas Sambanis, *Making War
and Building Peace: United Nations Peace Operations* (Princeton: Princeton University Press, 2006), 18.

2. Ibid., 350.

3. Ibid., 15.

4. Ibid., 305.

5. Ibid., 304.

6. Ibid., 307.

7. J. K. Gibson-Graham, *A Postcapitalist Politics* (Minneapolis: University of Minnesota Press, 2006), 194–95.

8. Doyle and Sambanis, *Making War and Building Peace*, 334–35.

9. Ibid., 335.

10. Ibid., 337.

11. Ibid., 338.

12. Nicholas Lemann, *Redemption: The Last Battle of the Civil War* (New York: Farrar, Straus, and Giroux, 2006), 185, 11, 27.

13. Doyle and Sambanis, *Making War and Building Peace*, 338.

14. Ibid., 200.

15. Ibid., 201, 205, 209.

16. John Paul Lederach, *The Moral Imagination: The Art and Soul of Building Peace* (New York: Oxford University Press, 2005), 46–49.

17. Ibid., 46–47.

18. Jos Havermans, "Lessons Learned from Ten Years Experience in Conflict Prevention: 'Every Conflict Is Unique, and So Is Its Solution,'" in *Towards Better Peacebuilding Practice: On Lessons Learned, Evaluation Practices and Aid and Conflict*, ed. Anneke Galama and Paul van Tongeren (Utrecht, Netherlands: European Centre for Conflict Prevention, 2002), 166–67.

19. Paul van Tongeren, "Inspiring Stories of Peacebuilding," in *People Building Peace: 35 Inspiring Stories from Around the World*, a publication of the European Centre for Conflict Prevention, in cooperation with the International Fellowship of Reconciliation and the Coexistence Initiative of State of the World Forum (Utrecht, Netherlands: European Centre for Conflict Prevention, 1999), 15.

20. Havermans, "Lessons Learned," 136.

21. Lederach, *Moral Imagination*, 54.

22. Ibid., 54, 84–85.

23. Ibid., 32.

3. Peacebuilding

1. Lisa Schirch, *The Little Book of Strategic Peacebuilding* (Intercourse, Pa.: Good Books, 2006), 89, 25–26.

2. Ibid., 9.

3. John Paul Lederach, *The Moral Imagination: The Art and Soul of Building Peace* (Oxford: Oxford University Press, 2005), 142–46.

4. Ikechi Mgbeoji, *Collective Insecurity: The Liberian Crisis, Unilateralism, and Global Order* (Vancouver: UBC, 2003), 80.

5. Quoted in Helene Poulet, "We Were Calling to Death," *Harper's Magazine*, February 2003, 14–15.

6. International Commission on Intervention and State Sovereignty, *The Responsibility to Protect: Report of the International Commission on Intervention and State Sovereignty* (Ottawa: International Development Research Centre, 2001), 40: 5.10.

7. Kees Kingma, "Demobilizing and Reintegrating Former Combatants," in *Peacebuilding: A Field Guide*, ed. Luc Reychler and Thania Paffenholz (Boulder: Lynne Rienner, 2001), 408, 414.

8. Schirch, *Strategic Peacebuilding*, 51–53.

9. Lederach, *Moral Imagination*, 143.

10. Ibid., 145.

11. Dan Bilefsky, "Bosnia Fugitive Remains a Hero to Some, a Butcher to Others," *New York Times*, August 5, 2008, A1, A11.

12. Michelle Parlevliet, "Telling the Truth in the Wake of Mass Violence," in *People Building Peace: 35 Inspiring Stories from Around the World*, a publication of the European Centre for Conflict Prevention, in cooperation with the International Fellowship of Reconciliation and the Coexistence Initiative of State of the World Forum (Utrecht, Netherlands: European Centre for Conflict Prevention, 1999), 47.

13. Lederach, *Moral Imagination*, 153, 176. See also Lisa Schirch, *Ritual and Symbol in Peacebuilding* (Sterling, Va.: Kumarian, 2005).

14. John Paul Lederach, *The Little Book of Conflict Transformation* (Intercourse, Pa.: Good Books, 2003), 3, 5, 14.

15. Ibid., 27.

16. International Commission on Intervention and State Sovereignty, *Responsibility to Protect*, 41: 5.14.

17. Sissela Bok, "Early Advocates of Lasting World Peace: Utopians or Realists?" in *Celebrating Peace*, ed. Leroy S. Rouner (Notre Dame: University of Indiana Press, 1990), 52–55.

18. "International Criminal Court," Citizens for Global Solutions (June 28, 2007), online at http://www.globalsolutions .org/issues/international_criminal_court (July 15, 2008).

19. Ibid.

20. International Criminal Court, online at http://www. icc-cpi.int/home.html&l=enwebsite (July 15, 2008).

21. "Publics around the World Say UN Has Responsibility to Protect against Genocide," Chicago Council on Global Affairs, worldpublicopinion.org (May 10, 2007); International Commission on Intervention and State Sovereignty, *Responsibility to Protect*, 3.29, 3.30.

22. Charlie Clements, *Witness to War* (New York: Bantam, 1984), 260–61.

23. Iris Marion Young, *Justice and the Politics of Difference* (Princeton, N.J.: Princeton University Press, 1990), 48.

24. Ibid., 52.

25. Ibid., 57.

26. Ibid., 60.

27. Ibid., 61.

28. M. K. Gandhi, *Non-violent Resistance (Satyagraha)* (New York: Schocken, 1951), 77, 87.

29. Ibid., 252.

30. Ibid., 77, 73, 87.

31. Ibid., 73–74.

32. Ibid., 386.

33. Ibid., 239.

34. Ibid., 81.

35. Ibid., 387.

36. Martin Luther King Jr., "An Experiment in Love," in *A Testament of Hope: The Essential Writings of Martin Luther King, Jr.*, ed. James M. Washington (Cambridge, Mass.: Harper & Row, 1986), 18.

37. Schirch, *Strategic Peacebuilding*, 28.

38. Ibid., 33.

39. Ibid., 31.

40. Schirch, *Strategic Peacebuilding*, 33.

41. Ibid., 30–33.

42. Camille Pampell Conaway and Anjalina Sen, *Beyond Conflict Prevention: How Women Prevent Violence and Build Sustainable Peace* (New York: Global Action to Prevent War and Women's International League for Peace and Freedom, 2005), 21–22.

43. Arjun Sengupta, "The Right to Development," in *Human Rights and the World Community: Issues and Action*, 3rd ed., ed. Richard Pierre Claude and Burns H. Weston (Philadelphia: University of Pennsylvania Press, 2006), 258–59. See also International Commission on Intervention and State Sovereignty, *Responsibility to Protect*, 42: 5.20.

44. International Commission on Intervention and State Sovereignty, *Responsibility to Protect*, 27: 3.23; 41: 5.15–18.

45. Schirch, *The Little Book of Strategic Peacebuilding*, 57.

46. Lederach, *Moral Imagination*, 43.

47. Schirch, *The Little Book of Strategic Peacebuilding*, 18, 20.

48. John Paul Lederach, *Building Peace: Sustainable Reconciliation in Divided Societies* (Washington, D.C.: United Institute of Peace Press, 1997), 91.

49. Schirch, *The Little Book of Strategic Peacebuilding*, 82.

50. Doyle and Sambanis, *Making War and Building Peace: United Nations Peace Operations* (Princeton: Princeton University Press, 2006), 57.

51. Lederach, *Moral Imagination*, 58.

52. Web sites: Global Action to Prevent War, online at www.globalactionpw.org; Friends Committee on National Legislation, online at www.fcnl.org/index.htm; Catholic Peacebuilding Network, online at http://cpn.nd.edu/.

53. James Dobbins, "Force and Enforcement: Alternatives to the Traditional Uses of Military Power," paper prepared for "Power and Superpower: Global Leadership for the 21st Century," a conference sponsored by the Security and Peace Initiative (New York: Century Foundation, 2006), 5.

54. Glen Stassen, ed., *Just Peacemaking: Ten Practices for Abolishing War*, 2nd ed. (Cleveland: Pilgrim, 2004).

55. Friends Committee on National Legislation, *Peaceful Prevention of Deadly Conflict: If War Is Not the Answer, What Is?* (Washington, D.C.: Friends Committee on National Legislation, 2004), 5.

56. In a conversation on October 16, 2006, Lisa Sowell Cahill, professor of ethics, described the convergence of people working on strategic peacebuilding. Rather than continue the principled debate between just war and pacifism, many scholars and activists are working together on the area where they do agree, the need for strategic peacebuilding: preventing war, resolving conflicts, and restoring conflict-torn societies. For an example of the range of participants and the topics addressed in such efforts, see the program for the twentieth-anniversary symposium of the Joan B. Kroc Institute for International Peace Studies at the University of Notre Dame, online at http://kroc.nd.edu/20conference.shtml (July 15, 2008).

4. Enduring Security

1. The September 2002 National Security Strategy of the United States of America can be accessed online at www.whitehouse.gov/nsc/nss.html (July 15, 2008).

2. Francis Fukuyama, *America at the Crossroads: Democracy, Power and the Neoconservative Legacy* (New Haven: Yale University Press, 2006), 9, 184–85, 10–11, 157, 161–64.

3. William Perry and Ashton Carter are codirectors of the Preventive Defense Project, a research collaboration of Stanford University and Harvard University's Kennedy School of Government, online at http://belfercenter.ksg.harvard.edu/project/2/preventive_defense_project.html?page_id=97 (September 6, 2008).

4. Joseph Nye Jr., *Soft Power: The Means to Succeed in World Politic*s (New York: Public Affairs, 2004), x, xi, 7.

5. Jonathan Schell, "Too Late for Empire," *The Nation*, August 14/21, 2006, 22.

6. William F. Schulz, *Tainted Legacy: 9/11 and the Ruin of Human Right*s (New York: Nation Books, 2003), 61.

7. Schell discusses Hannah Arendt's critique of totalitarianism in ch. 8 of *The Unconquerable World: Power, Nonviolence and the Will of the People* (New York: Metropolitan Books, 2003).

8. Michael R. Gordon gives a preview of this 2006 draft of the *Counterinsurgency Field Manuel* in an article for the *New York Times*: "Military Hones a New Strategy on Insurgency," October 5, 2006, A1, A19.

9. Quoted in Gordon, "Military Hones a New Strategy."

10. Gordon, "Military Hones a New Strategy."

11. Sarah Sewall, introduction to *The U.S. Army and Marine Corps Counterinsurgency Field Manual* (Chicago: University of Chicago Press, 2007), xxi.

12. Ibid., xxv.

13. Ibid., xxviii.

14. Lt. Colonel John Nagl, foreword to *Counterinsurgency Field Manual*, xxix.

15. Sewall, introduction to *Counterinsurgency Field Manual*, xxv, see also xxx.

16. *Counterinsurgency Field Manual*, 252. See also pp. 42–43, 245–52.

17. Sewall, introduction to *Counterinsurgency Field Manual*, xxvi.

18. Ibid., xxxvii.

19. The Dalai Lama, *Ethics for the New Millennium* (New York: Riverhead, 1999), 203.

20. Richard C. Leone and John Podesta, in their foreword to the collection of papers prepared for the conference entitled "Power and Superpower: Global Leadership for the 21st Century," sponsored by the Security and Peace Initiative, a joint initiative of the Center for American Progress and the Century Foundation (New York: Century Foundation, 2006), 1–2.

21. Mohandas K. Gandhi, "My Faith in Nonviolence (1930),"
in *The Power of Nonviolence: Writings by Advocates of Peace*,
ed. Howard Zinn (Boston: Beacon, 2002), 46.

22. Thomas Merton, "The Root of War Is Fear (1962)," in
Zinn, *Power of Nonviolence*, 97.

23. Theodore Parker, online at http://www.spiritus-temporis
.com/theodore-parker/final-words.html (September 6, 2008).

24. The mission and values of the American Friends Service
Committee are outlined on its Web site: http://www.afsc.org/
about/mission.htm (August 9, 2008).

25. Dietrich Bonhoeffer, "History and Good," in *Ethics*, ed.
Eberhard Bethge (New York: Macmillan, 1955), ch. 6.

26. Thomas King, *The Truth about Stories: A Native Narrative* (Minneapolis: University of Minnesota Press, 2003), 122.

27. Ibid., 77.

28. Ibid., 25.

29. Ibid., 25, 114.

30. Leslie Marmon Silko, *Ceremony* (New York: Penguin,
1977). Silko provides a chilling story of the destructive power
of the whites who come to the Americas: "They fear. / They
fear the world. / They destroy what they fear. / They fear themselves" (135).

31. King, *Truth about Stories*, 110.

32. Michael Hogue, *Varieties of Religious Ethics and the
Vulnerability of Life* (New York: Rowman & Littlefield, forthcoming), 3.

33. Ibid., 4.

34. Books on the topic of Engaged Buddhism that I have
found helpful include the following: Thich Nhat Hanh, *Being
Peace* (Berkeley: Parallax, 1987), 84; *Engaged Buddhism: Buddhist Liberation Movements in Asia*, ed. Christopher S. Queen
and Sallie B. King (Albany: State University of New York Press,
1996), 2–3; Kenneth Kraft, *The Wheel of Engaged Buddhism: A
New Map of the Path* (New York: Weatherhill, 1999); Kenneth
Kraft, ed., *Inner Peace, World Peace: Essays on Buddhism and
Nonviolence* (Albany, N.Y.: SUNY, 1992); Ken Jones, *The New
Social Face of Buddhism: An Alternative Sociopolitical Perspective* (Boston: Wisdom, 2003); David Loy, *The Great Awakening: A Buddhist Social Theory* (Boston: Wisdom, 2003).

35. Masao Abe, *Buddhism and Interfaith Dialogue*, ed. Steven Heine (Honolulu: University of Hawaii Press, 1995), 58–59.

36. Sister Annabel Laily, introduction to *Thich Nhat Hanh: Essential Writings*, ed. Robert Ellsburg (Maryknoll, N.Y.: Orbis, 2001), 7; Sulak Sivaraksa, *Seeds of Peace: A Buddhist Vision for Renewing Society*, ed. Tom Ginsburg (Berkeley: Parallax, 1992), 68.

37. Christopher S. Queen, "Introduction: A New Buddhism," in *Engaged Buddhism in the West* (Somerville, Mass.: Wisdom Publications, 2000), 2.

38. Stephen Batchelor, in *Engaged Buddhism in the West*, 413–14.

39. Kraft, *Wheel of Engaged Buddhism*, 20. Stephen Batchelor, *Buddhism without Beliefs: A Guide to Contemporary Awakening* (New York: Riverhead, 1997), 74, 89.

40. Abe, *Buddhism and Interfaith Dialogue*, 242.

41. Brian Victoria, *Zen at War* (New York: Weatherhill, 1997).

42. Masao Abe, *Zen and Western Thought*, ed. William R. LaFleur (Honolulu: University of Hawaii Press, 1985), 190.

43. Masao Abe, *Zen and Comparative Studies*, ed. Steven Heine (Honolulu: University of Hawaii Press, 1997), 37.

44. Abe, *Zen and Western Thought*, 190.

45. Stephen Batchelor, *Verses from the Center: A Buddhist Vision of the Sublime* (New York: Riverhead, 2000), 6.

46. Jones, *New Social Face of Buddhism*, 13.

47. Masao Abe, *Buddhism and Interfaith Dialogue*, 242.

48. Pema Chodron, *Practicing Peace in Times of War* (Boston: Shambala, 2006), 29.

49. Batchelor, *Buddhism without Beliefs*, 38.

50. Kraft, "New Voices in Engaged Buddhist Studies," in *Engaged Buddhism in the West*, ed. Christopher Queen, 497.

51. Thich Nhat Hanh, *Interbeing: Fourteen Guidelines for Engaged Buddhism*, 3rd ed. (Berkeley: Parallax, 1998), 17.

52. Stephanie Kaza and Kenneth Kraft, eds., *Dharma Rain: Sources of Buddhist Environmentalism* (Boston: Shambala, 2000), 7.

53. Kant, *Critique of Pure Reason*, trans. Norman Kemp Smith (New York: St. Martin's, 1965), 312.

54. Johann Baptist Metz, *Faith in History and Society: Toward a Practical Fundamental Theology* (New York: Crossroad, 2007), 105.

55. Jonathan Dean, "Some Reasons for Optimism," remarks from a forthcoming manuscript. Lecture delivered at the International Steering Committee Meeting of Global Action to Prevent War, Cuenca, Spain, January 26, 2005. Used with permission.

56. Ibid.

57. Michel Foucault, "Technologies of the Self," from a seminar given at the University of Vermont in October 1982, in *Ethics: Subjectivity and Truth*, Essential Works of Foucault (1954–1984), vol. 1, ed. Paul Rabinow (New York: New Press, 1997), 224–25.

58. "Structuralism and Post-structuralism," an interview conducted by Gerard Raulet, originally published in *Telos* 16: 55 (1983), 195–211, in *Aesthetics, Method and Epistemology*, ed. James D. Faubion, Essential Works of Foucault (1954–1984), vol. 2, ed. Paul Rabinow (New York: New Press, 1998), 449.

Additional Resources

Amnesty International
www.amnesty.org

"Founded in London in 1961, Amnesty International is a Nobel Prize-winning grassroots activist organization with over 1.8 million members worldwide. Amnesty International undertakes research and action focused on preventing and ending grave abuses of the rights to physical and mental integrity, freedom of conscience and expression, and freedom from discrimination, within the context of its work to promote all human rights."

Buddhist Peace Fellowship
www.bpf.org

"The mission of the Buddhist Peace Fellowship (BPF), founded in 1978, is to serve as a catalyst for socially engaged Buddhism. Our purpose is to help beings liberate themselves from the suffering that manifests in individuals, relationships, institutions, and social systems. BPF's programs, publications, and practice groups link Buddhist teachings of wisdom and compassion with progressive social change."

Catholic Peacebuilding Network
http://cpn.nd.edu/about_us.htm

"The Catholic Peacebuilding Network (CPN) is a voluntary net-work of practitioners, academics, clergy, and laity from around the world that seeks to enhance the study and practice of Cath-olic peacebuilding, especially at the local level. The CPN aims to deepen bonds of solidarity among Catholic peacebuilders, share and analyze "best practices," expand the peacebuilding capacity of the Church in areas of conflict, and encourage the further development of a theology of a just peace. While it is a Catholic network, the CPN believes that authentic and effective Catholic peacebuilding involves dialogue and collaboration with those of other religious traditions and all those committed to building a more just and peaceful world."

Eastern Mennonite University,
Center for Justice and Peacebuilding
www.emu.edu/cjp/

"CJP was founded to further the personal and professional development of individuals as peacebuilders and to strengthen the peacebuilding capacities of the institutions they serve."

Eastern Mennonite University, The 3D Security Initiative
www.3dsecurity.org

"3D security refers to the 3 pillars of foreign policy: develop-ment, diplomacy, and defense. The 3D Security Initiative takes a 3D approach to human and environmental security. We pro-mote conflict prevention and peacebuilding strategies to Mem-bers of Congress, the US military and the US public."

European Centre for Conflict Prevention
www.conflict-prevention.net

"[The ECCP is] a non-governmental organisation that pro-motes effective conflict prevention and peacebuilding strat-egies, and actively supports and connects people working for peace worldwide. Most of the ECCP's activities currently center on the Global Partnership for the Prevention of Armed Conflict (GPPAC), the network of which the ECCP holds the Global Secretariat."

Friends Committee on National Legislation
www.fcnl.org/about/

"The Friends Committee on National Legislation (FCNL) is the largest peace lobby in Washington, DC. Founded in 1943 by members of the Religious Society of Friends (Quakers), FCNL staff and volunteers work with a nationwide network of tens of thousands of people from many different races, religions, and cultures to advocate social and economic justice, peace, and good government. FCNL is nonpartisan."

Global Action to Prevent War
www.globalactionpw.org/index.htm

"Global Action to Prevent War is a transnational network of organizations and grassroots activists, active in over 53 countries. The coalition grounds the goal of conflict prevention in specific integrated phases of conflict prevention, peacekeeping and disarmament over a three to four decade period."

Human Security Report Project
www.humansecuritygateway.info/

"The Human Security Report provides updated information on continuing human security initiatives in the Human Security News. Human Security News is produced by the Human Security Centre at the Liu Institute for Global Issues at UBC. The Human Security Centre produces the annual Human Security Report and is funded by the governments of Canada, Norway, Sweden, Switzerland and the United Kingdom. For more information on human security visit the Human Security Gateway, an online research and information database that contains a broad range of human security-related resources."

Network of Spiritual Progressives:
A Project of the Tikkun Community
www.spiritualprogressives.org

The Network of Spiritual Progressives is an interfaith organization addressing issues of social justice, economic development, human rights, ecological responsibility and nonviolent conflict resolution.

Pace e Bene Nonviolence Service
http://paceebene.org/pace/

"Pace e Bene's mission is to develop the spirituality and practice of active nonviolence as a way of living and being and as a process for cultural transformation. Pace e Bene developed *Engage: Exploring Nonviolent Living,* a 12-session study program exploring and experimenting with nonviolence to address personal and social concerns."

Peacemaking: Congregational Study / Action Issue Resource Guide 2006–2010, Unitarian Universalist Association
www.uua.org/socialjustice/issuesprocess/currentissues/peacemaking/index.shtml

"The Congregational Study / Action Resource Guide provides tools for individuals and congregations to engage in a full exploration of violence and peacemaking on all levels. Resources include annotated bibliographies, curricula for all ages, teleseminars, and small group workshops."

Religions for Peace
www.wcrp.org

"Religions for Peace is the largest international coalition of representatives from the world's great religions dedicated to promoting peace."

Search for Common Ground
www.sfcg.org

"Founded in 1982, Search for Common Ground works to transform the way the world deals with conflict—away from adversarial approaches and towards collaborative problem solving. We work with local partners to find culturally appropriate means to strengthen societies' capacity to deal with conflicts constructively: to understand the differences and act on the commonalities."

United Nations Peace Operations
https://unp.un.org/details.aspx?pid=17907

Year in Review 2007: United Nations Peace Operations: "During a year in which the international community looked to the United Nations to launch peace operations in increasing numbers, size and complexity, the UN headquarters peace operations architecture underwent profound changes, with more to come, intended to enhance field work in conflict prevention, peacekeeping and peacebuilding. It has required that the UN seek ever more flexible, creative and cost-effective approaches. The changes and innovations begun in 2007 will certainly be tested as huge challenges remain in 2008 for resolving ongoing conflicts and preventing new ones. The publication presents an overview of innovations, expansion and restructuring as well as accomplishments and challenges of the UN peace operations during the year of 2007."

United Nations Peacebuilding Commission
www.un.org/peace/peacebuilding/

"The Peacebuilding Commission (PBC) is an intergovernmental advisory body of the United Nations that supports peace efforts in countries emerging from conflict, and is a key addition to the capacity of the International Community in the broad peace agenda."

Winning the Peace: Readings and Recommendations
for Post-conflict Operations
www.heritage.org/Research/NationalSecurity/SR07.cfm

Heritage Special Report. Published by The Heritage Foundation. SR-7 June 9, 2006.

"Since the end of the Cold War, the U.S. Armed Forces have been engaged in either a peacekeeping or post-conflict operation on average every two years. Operations in Iraq and Afghanistan have proved to be most difficult during the post-conflict stages. . . .

As a result of this strategic imperative, The Heritage Foundation has . . . [developed] a set of principles and recommendations that can be applied to post-conflict operations. The analyses in this report present a guide for building the kind of military America needs to secure its interests in the 21st century." Edwin J. Feulner, Ph.D., President, The Heritage Foundation.

The Women's International League for Peace and Freedom
www.wilpf.int.ch/AboutUs/index.htm

"The Women's International League for Peace and Freedom (WILPF) is an international Non Governmental Organization (NGO) with national sections, covering all continents with an international secretariat based in Geneva, and a New York office focused on the work of the United Nations. Since its establishment in 1915, WILPF has brought together women from around the world who are united in working for peace by non-violent means, promoting political, economic and social justice for all."